Perfect Days in

FUERTEVENTURA

Travel with Insider Tips

www.marco-polo.com

Contents

⭐ **TOP 10** 4

That Fuerteventura Feeling 6

9 The Magazine
The Desert Island ■ Guanches, Majores and Conquistadores ■ Catch a Wave ■ Carnival and Fiesta ■ Food and Drink ■ Family Fun on Fuerteventura ■ Where the Wild Things Are ■ Life in the Seas ■ Shipwrecks ■ My Fuerteventura

35 Finding Your Feet
■ First Two Hours
■ Getting Around
■ Accommodation
■ Food and Drink
■ Shopping
■ Entertainment

43 The North
Getting Your Bearings ■ **Four Perfect Days**
TOP 10 ■ Isla de Lobos ■ Corralejo ■ La Oliva
At Your Leisure ■ More Places to Explore
Where to... ■ Eat and Drink ■ Stay ■ Shop ■ Go Out

65 The Centre
Getting Your Bearings ■ **Two Perfect Days**
TOP 10 ■ Betancuria ■ Antigua ■ Ecomuseo de La Alcogida
At Your Leisure ■ More Places to Explore
Where to... ■ Eat and Drink ■ Stay ■ Shop ■ Go Out

85 The South
Getting Your Bearings ■ **Three Perfect Days**
TOP 10 ■ Playas de Jandía ■ La Lajita Oasis Park
At Your Leisure ■ More Places to Explore
Where to... ■ Eat and Drink ■ Stay ■ Shop ■ Go Out

107 Lanzarote
Getting Your Bearings ■ **The Perfect Day**
TOP 10 ■ Parque Nacional de Timanfaya ■ Jameos del Agua
Don't Miss ■ Teguise
At Your Leisure ■ More Places to Explore
Where to... ■ Eat and Drink ■ Stay ■ Shop ■ Go Out

127 Gran Canaria
Getting Your Bearings ■ **Seven Perfect Days**
Don't Miss ■ Casa de Colón ■ Museo Canario
At Your Leisure ■ More Places to Explore
Where to... ■ Eat and Drink ■ Stay ■ Shop ■ Go Out

137 Walks & Tours
■ 1 Isla de Lobos
■ 2 Sendero de Bayuyo
■ 3 Highlights in North and Central Fuerteventura
■ 4 Coast-to-Coast

Practicalities 153
■ Before You Go
■ When You are There
■ Useful Words and Phrases

Road Atlas 161

Index 173

Picture Credits 176

Credits 177

10 Reasons to Come Back Again 178

For chapters: see inside front cover

★ TOP 10

Not to be missed!
Our TOP 10 hits – from the absolute No. 1 to No. 10 –
help you plan your tour of the most important sights.

★ PLAYAS DE JANDÍA ▶ 90
Fuerteventura's beach paradise is the main reason that millions of tourists flock to this island in the sun every year.

★ BETANCURIA ▶ 70
Located inland, away from the sea, the old capital retains its colonial flair and is one of the most popular day-trip destinations on the island.

★ ANTIGUA ▶ 73
A windmill (ill. left) forms the hub of a museum complex that also includes a botanical garden and a crafts centre.

★ ISLA DE LOBOS ▶ 48
It is possible to explore the uninhabited island just off the north coast by booking a boat trip combined with a short walking tour. The highlight is climbing the Montaña Caldera volcano.

★ CORRALEJO ▶ 50
A popular holiday destination on the north of the island is Corralejo; stretching along the coast to the south is a magnificent dune and beach landscape. At sunrise, the dunes look absolutely amazing.

★ LA OLIVA ▶ 53
In the north, the fortified Casa del los Coroneles provides an excellent view of the island's turbulent past.

★ ECOMUSEO DE LA ALCOGIDA ▶ 74
In the intricately and lovingly designed open-air museum, five beautifully restored farmhouses and *artesanías* demonstrate how the rural population used to live.

★ OASIS PARK ▶ 93
The large zoo, embedded in what for Fuerteventura could almost be classed as lush subtropical vegetation, is a favourite with children for its sea lion and reptile shows.

★ PARQUE NACIONAL TIMANFAYA ▶ 114
A day trip to the neighbouring island of Lanzarote introduces you to the wonderful volcanic legacy of the Canary Islands.

★ JAMEOS DEL AGUA ▶ 116
The highlights of the fantasy grotto created by César Manrique inside this lava tube are a Caribbean-style pool and a cave-based auditorium famous for its fantastic acoustics.

THAT FUERTEVENTURA

Find out what makes the island tick, experience its unique flair – just like the *majoreros* themselves.

WIND AND WAVES

Visit Fuerteventura, and you will experience the sea at its best. You will not find such broad open beaches on any of the other Canary Islands. Granted, a few of them are slightly disfigured by unattractive hotel complexes, but on the unspoiled **Playa de Barlovento** (➤ 91), you can sometimes walk for hours barefoot along the edge of the water without meeting a soul, enjoying the sea breeze, the lapping of the waves against the shore and the screeching of the seagulls circling above you.

PURE RELAXATION

The **South** (➤ 85) of Fuerteventura, from Costa Calma to Morro Jable, is still relatively uncharted territory for tourists. Just 40 years ago, apart from two tiny fishing hamlets, there was practically no tourist infrastructure here at all. It still does not have any cultural highlights for your photo album, but you can swim, surf, dive, wander along the beaches, meditate or simply relax by the hotel pool and read a novel.

SAHARA FEELING

The **dunes of Corralejo** (➤ 52) save you a trip to the Sahara. The constant wind has piled up towering hills of sand, which offer a particularly impressive view of the wonders of nature on a morning walk or in the soft light just before sunset. Against this background, the tall Riu hotels – built in the 1970s when this expansive area was not yet protected – give the impression of a Fata Morgana mirage.

VOLCANO WALK

You are missing something if you regard Fuerteventura as just a beach holiday destination. There are countless wonderful ways to explore the island on foot. For instance, the well marked **Sendero de Bayuyo** (➤ 142) trail leads you on an excursion through the bizarre Malpaís de Bayuyo lava field. You can view the volcanic

FEELING

A dream island: sandy beaches, sea and volcanic mountains by Corralejo

That Fuerteventura Feeling

past of the island first-hand and look down into the crater of Calderón Hondo.

WATERFRONT RESTAURANT

What could be nicer after enjoying some sun and sand than to round off the day in a fish restaurant? There are plenty of places to do this along the 300km (186mi)-long coast around Fuerteventura. The largest choice is offered on the promenade of Morro Jable which is lined with restaurants; you are in good hands at the **Blue Marlin** (➤ 102), where fish is baked in a delicious salt crust.

COLONIAL FLAIR

Compared with the main islands of Gran Canaria and Tenerife, the colonial heritage on Fuerteventura is relatively modest. Yet in some places, the past is still alive here, too, especially in the old capital of **Betancuria** (➤ 70). There, you enter the parish church through an attractive Renaissance portal, and cosy restaurants have been set up in the old mansion houses.

SAY CHEESE

Until just a few years ago, there were more goats than humans living on Fuerteventura. Even today, of all the Canary Islands, Fuerte remains the one associated with goats. The much prized goat's cheese is extremely popular in many of the restaurants. It usually comes fried and with *mojo* sauce. Refined with sweet paprika or gofio, the cheese has a unique flavour. Sometimes it is also smoked and served together with air-dried ham. A good place to sample the different varieties is in the Betancuria cheese factory (➤ 83).

Casa Santa Maria: one of the best restaurants in the island's old capital Betancuria

The Magazine

The Desert Island	10
Guanches, Majores and Conquistadores	13
Catch a Wave	16
Carnival and Fiesta	19
Food and Drink	22
Family Fun on Fuerteventura	26
Where the Wild Things Are	28
Life in the Seas	30
Shipwrecks	32
My Fuerteventura	34

The **DESERT** Island

Of all the Canaries, Fuerteventura is the classic desert island. It is often referred to as "a little bit of Sahara which has chipped off the coast of Africa", and while that is geologically incorrect – like all the Canaries it was born from underwater volcanic explosions – it does convey a good deal of the character of Fuerteventura.

Even the golden yellow sand on the beaches was not, as is often incorrectly claimed, blown over from the Sahara but is actually "home-made".

For visitors much of the island offers a magnificent untamed natural beauty: ancient mountain ranges and volcanic cones trimmed by deep dry *barrancos* (ravines), and coastlines either softened by Saharan dunes or battered by the elements into bizarre shapes. Less attractively, there are also great stretches of volcanic *malpais* (literally, badlands), black areas of scorched, cracked earth where nothing more than lichens grow. For the islanders this has always been a harsh, unforgiving climate in which to eke a living. However, *majoreros*, as the people of Fuerteventura are colloquially known, are nothing if not resourceful. In the fields the wind has been harnessed to power hundreds of *molinos* (conventional windmills), *molinas* (windmills mounted on top of buildings), steel water pumps and wind

Left: A barren landscape of volcanic origin; above: instead of tomatoes, the Canarios now cultivate aloe vera, as seen here in a field in the Valles de Ortega

turbines. In the burning sun, aloe vera and some Sisal flourish, while the former wide-spread cultivation of tomatoes has more or less been abandoned. It is no wonder that goats are so prized in a landscape that would support few other kinds of fussier creature. Until quite recently, that most durable of all land animals, the camel, was a familiar island workhorse; today it tends to be more of a tourist attraction.

Fishermen in particular are at the mercy of the elements – the often-visible wrecks of ocean-going vessels weighing many thousands of tons are testimony to the power of the Atlantic – and on the west coast the fishing fleets operate only during the summer season.

Meeting new challenges

Yet times are changing. A 1960s guidebook to Lanzarote referred to Fuerteventura as being poverty-stricken but today the beaches of Corralejo are filled with visitors who spend hundreds of euros on kiteboarding courses, enjoy slap-up meals in the town's many restaurants and then retire to be pampered in luxury at their four- and five-star hotels.

Having managed to survive on a basic economy since before the days of the

WHERE IS EVERYONE?

With an average population density of just 12 people per square kilometre, Fuerteventura is easily the emptiest of the Canary Islands. Much of the island's west coast is deserted and accessible only by tracks, and the northern part of the Jandía peninsula is unpopulated except for the single ramshackle hamlet of Cofete. This is good news for naturists and away from the resorts most beaches are "clothing optional".

The increasing number of visitors is presenting Fuerteventura with new challenges; yet at the moment everyday life still continues as it always has, even in Corralejo

Conquest, the islanders' latest challenge is how to reap the benefits of tourism without sowing the seeds of cultural destruction. The success of *casas rurales* and *hoteles rurales* (rural guesthouses and hotels), as well as projects such as the Ecomuseo de La Alcogida open-air museum, are seen by many to be the most appropriate routes for controlled tourist development. Yet the growing number of holiday resorts in tourist magnets such as El Cotillo and Corralejo, not to mention the plans for hollowing out the island's most sacred mountain as a tourist attraction, are of great concern to many islanders and Canarian conservationists. For the moment, at least, most of Fuerteventura remains, in the words of the poet Miguel Unamuno, "an oasis in the desert of civilization".

LANGOSTAS ON THE MENU

It is not only sand that blows across from the Sahara. Migratory birds are blown off course and end up here along with swarms of locusts *(langostas)*. Millions descended on the island in 2004, and while they are harmless to humans directly, they do of course devastate crops, and have a deterrent effect on tourism. It is possible to turn the tables on these voracious creatures, however, and official leaflets distributed in 2004 on how to deal with the creatures even included a couple of recipes – apparently they are quite tasty when fried in garlic!

The Magazine

GUANCHES, MAJORES and CONQUISTADORES

When the Norman baron Jean de Béthencourt first arrived on Fuerteventura in 1402, a curious sight awaited him. Here were a people only slightly removed from the Stone Age in appearance and technology.

They lived together, just a few hundred strong, in primitive societies with basic laws and rough draconian justice; convicted criminals' skulls were crushed by heavy rocks, for example. Yet it is also recorded that they were a peaceful people with high moral standards; Béthencourt's priests chronicled, "go throughout the world and nowhere will you find a finer and better formed people…with great minds were they to receive instructions" (Bontier & le Verrier, tr. and ed, *Le Canarien*, 1872).

The history books came to call them Guanches ("gwanches") but in fact this term is a general one for any aboriginal Canary Island dweller and the ancient people of Fuerteventura came to be known as *majoreros* (pronounced "ma-ho-rair-os") or Mahohreros, possibly named after the particular types of caves *(majos)* that they built, or from the word *mahos* meaning a type of goatskin shoe which they wore.

The origin of the Guanches

It is thought that these original islanders were of Berber origin, coming from Morocco in Roman times (carbon-dating points to the 1st or 2nd century bc) and they may have been from the Canarii tribe, hence the subsequent name of the archipelago.

WHAT'S IN A NAME?

The island's original name was Erbania, probably referring to the wall (*bani* in the Berber language) that divided the kingdoms. The first mention of Forte Ventura appears on a map in 1339. Popular legend has it that when Béthencourt landed he uttered the words, "*Que fuerte ventura*" ("What great fortune/luck"). But more prosaically it probably refers to the island's strong winds.

13

The Magazine

They dwelt in caves and in low houses (as many villagers do today), kept goats, ate shellfish and grain, made simple pottery and tattooed themselves in geometrical patterns with pottery stamps known as *pintaderas*. These were probably also used to distinguish ownership of pots in grain stores.

The island was divided into two kingdoms: Jandía (as it is today), ruled by King Guize, and Maxorata (the rest of the island), ruled by King Ayoze. Béthencourt recorded that a low wall, around a metre high, crossed the island at La Pared dividing the two kingdoms. Traces of it can still be found today and there may have been defensive turrets in place.

Spain's gain

Had the French court supported the Norman explorer Jean de Béthencourt, the inhabitants of the Canary Islands would probably be speaking French today. However, the French refused to finance Béthencourt's project and thus the knight took his request to Castile. There, he was told that he would receive support only if the islands subsequently became part of the Spanish empire.

A reconstruction of the painted Cueva Pintada is on display at the Museo Canario on Fuerteventura's neighbouring island of Gran Canaria

The Magazine

INSIDER INFO

Compared with the islands of Gran Canaria and La Palma, the original inhabitants of Fuerteventura have left few traces. The vast majority of these are hidden away or inaccessible to the average visitor. Objects found in the cave at Villaverde may be seen in the Museo Arqueológico at Betancuria (► 72) but the best-known site associated with the ancients is Montaña Tindaya (► 57) with rock carvings at the summit. The Museo Canario in Las Palmas de Gran Canaria (► 133) offers the most extensive exhibition of this ancient culture.

Insider Tip

Béthencourt thus travelled to the islands, to discover new land and resources for Castile. The job of the missionaries accompanying him was to convert the natives to Christianity. Frustrated in meeting either of these aims and meeting strong resistance from the islanders, the French nobleman sailed back to his Castilian sponsors for reinforcements.

Fuerteventura becomes an outpost of Castile

When Béthencourt returned with his conquistadors in 1404 he found that the islanders had built forts at Valtarajal (later known as Betancuria) and Rico Roque (close to El Cotillo), but armed with merely spears and staves against guns they were soon overcome. Some fled into the mountains before giving themselves up to be sold into slavery abroad. Many died of common diseases imported by the invaders. In January 1405, the two kings surrendered and the remaining islanders followed their example. They were allowed to live and the kings were even given part of their lands back. However, Fuerteventura was now an outpost of Castile.

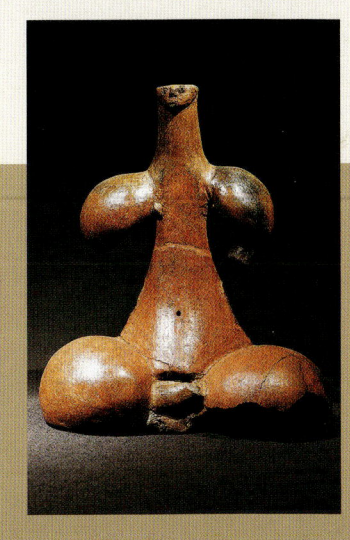

The Idol of Tara is an artwork produced by the Guanches. Found on Gran Canaria, the clay statue is also on view in the Museo Canario

15

The Magazine

Catch a WAVE

Ask anyone who has ever ridden a board across the waves and they will tell you Fuerteventura is one of the best places in the world for windsurfing.

It's basically down to geography. The Canary Islands have always benefited (and suffered) from heavy swells and strong winds. Ancient mariners relied on these "trade winds" to speed their voyages, and water sports fans also look for strong and reliable breezes. This is where the "acceleration zones" come in. These occur where the wind is funnelled between mountains or small islands and can triple the wind in strength. Because of its location, Fuerteventura – in particular the Sotavento coast of Jandía and the northern coast around Corralejo – benefits from this effect.

Windsurfing, the island's top sport

Windsurfing is the number one sport on the island and in July 1986 the first Windsurfing World Cup competition was held on Sotavento Beach. In 2001, it became the Windsurfing and Kiteboarding World Cup in recognition of this exciting new development in water sports. Kitesurfing or kiteboarding began in its present form in the late 1990s and has been described as a cross between windsurfing, wakeboarding and paragliding. Kitesurfers control a wing of lightweight fabric, which pulls them across the water at speeds of up to 70kph (43mph). The experts can fly up to 15m (50ft) high in the air performing all manner of gymnastics before coming down again some 70m from where they first took off.

> **INSIDER INFO**
>
> Advanced windsurfers should come in summer when the winds race hard from the high-pressure areas in the Azores to the low-pressure zone in the Sahara. Novices will be better off visiting in winter.

The Magazine

Windsurfing for beginners

A couple of hours spent typically in a quiet waist-deep lagoon setting will set you back around €60. A three-day course will cost around €120. After that you should have an idea if you like it or not and can sign on for progressively longer courses and/or hire your own rig (board and sail).

Surfing

Fuerteventura is also renowned for its surfing conditions, which are best during the winter months (October to March) when there is less wind and the waves are bigger.

There are a number of surfing schools on the island. On the north coast in Corralejo, the team from Islandboarders (www.islandboarderssurfschool.com) has 20 years of experience in this area. A one-day course costs €45 and consists of a four-hour session involving safety, paddling and standing techniques. The beginner's course (€110) aims to have you standing after three days. You will spend three to four hours in the water everyday learning standing techniques, board control, paddling and wipe out survival, plus theory lessons on types of breaks, surf-board design, equipment, history and water survival and safety.

Above: Surfers on the north-west coast
Below: Trade winds and the big waves make Fuerteventura a surfer's paradise

The broad beaches of Corralejo are a paradise for kiteboarders

Another reputable school is Quiksilver Surf School, also based at Corralejo. It was founded in 1994 by Joachim Hirsch, German longboard champion in 1999 and former member of the German national surf team – see www.quiksilver-surfschool.com.

In the south, surfers will also find excellent conditions off the coast at La Pared. There are also a number of schools that offer "surf camps", such as the team from Waveguru (www.waveguru.de/en). And, of course. stand-up paddle surfing arrived in Fuerteventura some time ago. You can hire boards for this trendy, easy-to-learn sport from many places along the coast.

Kitesurfing

Despite what you may think, you don't have to be a surfer of any kind to start kitesurfing, though of course it helps. In fact it's more important at the outset that you can handle a stunt kite properly and understand the nature of the wind. Neither do you need a great deal of strength, as the harness will take the strain off your arms. An introductory eight-hour course costs around €230.

Top Operators are Flag Beach Windsurf and Kitesurf Centre, Corralejo (▶ 64) and Pro Center René Egli K2 Watersports Centre, Sotavento Beach, Jandía (▶ 106)

It is not easy to start with.
But don't be disheartened!

The Magazine

CARNIVAL
and FIESTA

The Canary Islands celebrate the traditional pre-Lent carnival, or *carnaval* as it is known in Spain, with every ounce of energy they can muster. Gran Canaria and Tenerife compete to stage the biggest parades this side of Rio, while the other islands do their very best to keep pace.

The biggest *carnaval* celebrations on Fuerteventura are in Corralejo and Puerto del Rosario, though it is celebrated with gusto all over the island. The dates vary from year to year, but it all starts around nine weeks before Easter (usually early to mid-February) with the *Verbena de la Sábana* (Sheet Party) for which participants dress in a sheet and little else. After this the Carnival Queen and the Children's Queen are elected.

The climax of festivities is the Friday before Shrove Tuesday, when the Carnival Drag Queen is chosen, and the next day, when the grand parade of dozens of colourful floats takes place. Street parties and processions shimmy and shake to the insistent beat of salsa, lubricated by a seemingly inexhaustible supply of *cuba libre* (rum, cola, lime juice and ice) served from street kiosks.

Everyone puts on fancy dress and parties in the street

The Burial of the Sardine

A feature of *carnaval* is that men always dress in drag. If you think that is odd wait until you see the strangest ceremony of all, the Burial of the Sardine, which symbolises the end of *carnaval* and the beginning of Lent, as well as the Lenten fast and abstinence. On Ash Wednesday a huge papier-maché sardine is carried in mock funeral procession through the streets accompanied by the bizarre sight and sound of black-clad "mourners" wailing and crying. When the sardine arrives at its appointed place at the harbour, fireworks inside the fish are lit and it is literally blown to pieces.

Festivities in honour of the Virgin Mary

Island fiestas commemorate the feast day of the local saint or the Virgin/Our Lady, *(Nuestra Señora).* The centrepiece is a procession with

INSIDER INFO

If you know you will be in Fuerteventura during *carnaval* time be prepared to party and bring along some fancy dress – anything will do, the more colourful and more outlandish the better.

If you really want to see how Canarians can celebrate *carnaval* catch a plane to Las Palmas (▶ 127) on Gran Canaria or Tenerife, where the really large processions take place. See www.fuerteventura.com for dates and details of events.

The most spectacular processions take place on Gran Canaria and Tenerife (left); festive mood at the Fiesta de la Virgen del Pino on Gran Canaria (above)

prominent parishioners carrying an effigy of the saint or the Virgin shoulder-high through the streets accompanied by troupes of local musicians in traditional dress. The more important fiestas will also have carnival-style floats, street food and stalls, and culminate in fireworks. One of the island's most important fiestas is the Romería (pilgrimage) to the Ermita of the Virgen de la Peña, the patron saint of the island, in Vega de Río Palmas on the third weekend in September.

The Fiesta de Nuestra Señora del Carmen on 16 July at Corralejo and Morro Jable pays homage to the patron saint of fishermen with colourful boat processions led by local fishermen carrying a statue of the Virgin.

On the third Sunday in August, the old harbour at El Cotillo is dotted with boats celebrating Nuestra Señora del Buen Viaje. The Fiesta de la Virgen del Pino is always on 8 September on Gran Canaria.

FUERTEVENTURA 1 ENGLAND 0

On 13 October the locals celebrate the day they gave the English a bloody nose in 1740 by re-enacting the Battle of Tamasite, near Tuineje. A troop of well-armed English privateers (state-sanctioned pirates) attacked near Tuineje and was seen off by a group of 37 locals with muskets and agricultural tools. Thirty Englishmen were killed and five locals died. A cannon was captured and is on display outside the archaeological museum in Betancuria. A painting in the church of Tuineje also recalls the victory.

The Magazine

FOOD and DRINK

Genuine Canarian cuisine is all about dishes that originated in the kitchens of peasants and fishermen, as typified by hearty stews and simple barbecued fish. International and particularly anglicised meals may be the staple menu in holiday resorts.

The majority of restaurants on the island still serve a mix of Spanish and Canarian food. Start off with *tapas*, a concept imported from the Spanish mainland, and you have a meal that is as interesting, colourful and satisfying as in any European holiday destination.

Mojo and papas

The Canary Islands' most distinctive tastes are *mojo picón* and *mojo verde*. *Mojo picón* (literally "piquant sauce") is made from chilli peppers, garlic, cumin, paprika and vinegar. It is served cold and normally accompanies meat dishes and *papas arrugadas*. The latter (literally "wrinkly potatoes")

Stop for a tapas snack

The Magazine

is another Canarian staple – small new potatoes boiled in salty water and served with a generous sprinkling of sea salt. They are nearly always delicious and rarely taste too salty. By contrast to the fiery red variety, *mojo verde* (green sauce) is a cool fresh blend substituting coriander for chilli, and always accompanies fish.

Island specials: meat and cheese

The goat is the symbol of Fuerteventura (▶ 28) and appears on the menu in just about every conceivable form. Most local restaurants have goat's cheese *(queso de cabra)* among their starters, usually with sliced tomatoes. It may also be fried in breadcrumbs and served with quince jam *(membrillo)*, palm honey *(miel de palma)* or perhaps *mojo verde*. Look under "specialities" for *cabrito* (kid), which is either fried, baked or served in a stew *(compuesta)*. Another goat dish is *higado de cabra frita* (fried goat liver). Some restaurants only serve goat or kid stew on a Sunday lunchtime and specify that it must be ordered in advance. *Conejo* (rabbit) is also popular, served either in a tomato stew *(al salmorejo)* or perhaps fried *(frito)*.

South American specials

The close ties that have developed over the years with Venezuela, due to the *Canarios* moving back and forth, are reflected in the dishes served on the island. In many of the bars you will find *Arepas*, sandwiches of flat bread made of ground corn dough, filled with meat, such as chicken, or as a vegetarian option with vegetables and goat's cheese and then baked to become a crispy snack. Even the *Empanadas* (stuffed pastries), which actually originate from Argentina, can be found in many places.

TASTY TAPAS AND STARTERS

Albóndigas – meatballs

Calamares – fried battered squid

Chorizos al vino tinto – paprika sausage in red wine

Croquetas – croquettes, which may be filled with potatoes

Gambas – prawns

Jamón serrano – mountain cured ham. *Pata negra* is the best variety, though very expensive.

Mejillones – mussels

Pimientos – peppers. These may be stuffed with a variety of fillings. They are sometimes served smothered in melted cheese.

Pulpo – octopus

Tortilla – potato omelette

The Magazine

Island fish

The cheapest fish on most local restaurant menus is *corvina* (black drum) but it's usually worth paying a bit more for *cherne* (grouper), *vieja* (parrotfish), *sama* (sea bream) or *gallo* (John Dory). Other local fish and seafood items include *atún* (tuna), *pez espada* (swordfish), *merluza* (hake) and *lenguado* (sole). Ever popular is that sizzling Spanish starter *gambas al ajillo* (prawns in garlic sauce). Paella, Spain's national dish, typically including mussels, prawns and often rabbit, is very popular.

Sweet things

In traditional local establishments the choice of *postres* (desserts) is usually restricted to flan (the ubiquitous Spanish crème caramel) or *helado* (ice cream). However, in the new wave of Spanish-Canarian restaurants keep an eye out for some of the following: home-made cheesecake; home-made apple cake; *frangollo* (made of gofio – see below – and dried fruit soaked in syrup); *bienmesabe* (ground almonds, egg yolks and sugar syrup blended to the consistency of honey), often served with ice cream or bananas; *leche asada* (literally "baked milk", a kind of lemony sponge milk pudding); and *leche frita* ("fried milk"), also like crème caramel.

Vegetarian vicissitudes

Fish aside, it's hard to get a true vegetarian meal in a local restaurant. Even dishes like *potaje de berros* (watercress soup) or *garbanzos compuestos* (chickpea stew) include bacon or pork. Restaurants with Canarian cuisine rarely have a vegetarian menu; however, Italian and Asian restaurants offer a good alternative.

Gofio – the staff of life

Gofio, flour made by grinding toasted barley, corn or wheat, has been the Canarian staple

From top: You can order paella and papas arrugadas everywhere. Equally delicious: seafood and Canarian wine

The Magazine

since Guanche times (▶ 13). It is typically eaten by islanders as porridge or as a kind of polenta, or used to thicken soups and stews. It also occasionally finds its way onto the tourist menu under *gofio escaldado* (combined with fish stock), *helado de gofio* (ice cream) or perhaps *mousse de gofio*.

And to drink…
Fuerteventura produces small quantities of its own wine but most table wine is from mainland Spain, Tenerife or Lanzarote. Try also *ronmiel* ("honey rum"), a Canarian speciality made with palm honey. A guide to drinking ▶ 41.

Snacking
Go into even the humblest corner café and they will be pleased to serve you a satisfying *bocadillo de lomo* (pork loin sandwich in French bread), which automatically comes with cheese and tomato. Tapas bars are as common as they are on the Spanish mainland and offer delicious titbits between main meals.

More Canarian specialities
Potaje or *puchero canario* – a hearty meat and vegetable casserole, which may be served with *gofio* dumplings.
Rancho canario – a stew of meat, potatoes, chickpeas, tomatoes and noodles.
Ropa vieja – literally "old clothes", a stew of meat, chickpeas and whatever vegetables the chef throws in.
Sancocho – salt fish and potato stew.

Julian Diaz shows off some of the goat's cheese in his shop in Tiscamanita

The Magazine

Family **FUN**
ON FUERTEVENTURA

With its mile upon mile of sandy beaches, Fuerteventura is a delight for young children and perfect for older ones who may wish to start their first water sports lessons here.

Windsurfing
Children's windsurfing tuition begins at ten years old. Flag Beach in the north (➤ 64), René Egli in the south (➤ 106), and Fanatic Fun Centre in Caleta de Fuste are recommended operators. Beginners are taught in calm lagoon conditions: at Risco del Paso in the south; at El Cotillo in the north; and on the calm beach of Caleta de Fuste.

Surfing
Bodyboarding, or boogie boarding as it is also known, is the first step towards learning to surf, and kids can start this as soon as they are confident in the water. Shops all over the island sell bodyboards. The main beaches for surfing are El Cotillo, Corralejo and La Pared. Good

Sun, sand and water: Children only need a handkerchief-sized piece of sand to have fun

The Magazine

INSIDER INFO

If your children enjoy seeing birds and animals – there are also shows and camel rides – then Oasis Park at La Lajita (➤ 93) is a *Insider Tip* perfect day out in a tropical garden setting. The island's only water park is in Corralejo at the Baku complex (➤ 50), which also includes a whole host of other family entertainments.

There are tenpin bowling alleys at Caleta de Fuste and at Corralejo.

surfboarding schools are Islandboarders and Quiksilver Surf School, both at Corralejo, and tuition for children begins at the age of ten.

Scuba-diving
The minimum age for diving is ten years old. Recommended schools in Corralejo are Corralejo Dive Centre and the Punta Amanay Dive Centre (➤ 31).

Go fly a kite
Second only in colour to *carnaval* is the International Kite Festival which has been held in the dunes of Corralejo on the second weekend of October each year since 1992. The best kite fliers in Europe take part and the highlight is the Night Fly on Saturday night when illuminated kites create a mesmerising performance. Anyone can join in on the Friday when expert instructors are on hand. Just bring a kite – the more colourful the better – and you will be very welcome.

Beaches and adventure
Isla de Lobos (➤ 48) is an excellent day out for children. Older ones can be desert island explorers, little ones can play safely in the warm shallows of a soft golden sandy cove. If you need parasols, lounge beds, snack bars, showers and toilets on the beach, then there's only a limited choice of where to go. Corralejo, Caleta de Fuste, Costa Calma and Morro Jable are well-equipped popular family choices. Many beaches have few facilities so go prepared and always have your own shade to hand. The best beaches for little ones are Playa de la Concha at Isla de Lobos and the lagoon beaches at El Cotillo.

Where the **WILD THINGS** Are

Fuerteventura may not have a great choice of indigenous animals but there are three local creatures that almost every visitor will meet!

If Fuerteventura has a national animal it is the goat *(cabra)*. These hardy creatures can scavenge a meal from the meanest terrain, from thorny bushes in rocky outcrops to scrubby foliage among the sand dunes. They total around 60,000 strong, almost as many as the island's resident human population. Goats have been herded since Guanche times and at one time or another most parts of this creature have been put to some practical use. Goat meat and cheese feature prominently on all local restaurant menus, their skins were once used for clothing and their stomachs were used for bags in which *gofio* (➤ 24) was stored.

In total there are more than 30 different types of goats on the island. These range from the plain *blanca* (white) and *negro* (black) varieties to the dapple-coated *puipana colorada*, and from cute little kids to huge horned beasts. The hill countryside around Betancuria (➤ 70) is a good place to check them out.

Camels

The camel, or rather the single-humped dromedary, was introduced to the island in 1405 by the Normans and, being the most efficient creature

There are around 300 camels on the island (left) and numerous squirrels (above)

in this harsh dry terrain, was used in the fields and as a beast of burden right up until the 1950s. In the 16th century there were 4,000 camels on Fuerteventura, but by 1985 there were less than 30. Nowadays, thanks to tourism and the breeding scheme at Oasis Park (➤ 93–95), numbers have recovered to around 300 and Oasis Park has plans to set up the first camel milk dairy in Europe. Camel milk has as much protein but 40 per cent less cholesterol than cow's milk and a high mineral and vitamin C content.

Barbary ground squirrels

Erroneously described as chipmunks, these cute little critters look like a cross between a chipmunk and a grey squirrel and can be seen scuttling almost anywhere on the island where food is being handed out, be it on the promenade in Morro Jable or at the *miradores* of the interior. They are good fun and very tame but it's really not a good idea to feed them as, among other things, this interferes with their natural food-gathering instincts.

BEWARE LEAPING GOATS!

Traffic signs that seem to depict a graceful leaping deer in a red triangle are in fact warning you to beware of the goats.

The reason that the sign bears little resemblance to a goat is that it was designed with deer in mind and the Fuerteventura authorities simply bought them "off-the-peg" as the nearest thing!

The Magazine
Life in the SEAS

The climate, clear volcanic sea beds and depths of up to 3,500m (11,500ft) make the Canarian archipelago ideal for diving and deep-sea fishing.

There is an enormous variety of fish to be caught, including rays, sharks, swordfish, albacora, big-eye, yellow fin and skipjack tuna, bonito, barracuda, wahoo, and the most prestigious and feistiest prize of all, blue marlin. No previous experience is required. All catches belong to the skipper, though most big-game fish are tagged and released. A day's deep-sea fishing, which usually lasts around six hours, costs around €50 per person and there are operators on the quaysides at Caleta de Fuste, Corralejo and Morro Jable.

Whale and dolphin spotting

While it is feasible to spot whales, dolphins, flying fish and turtles on any sea voyage from Fuerteventura, there are two trips dedicated to spotting

Divers and snorkellers delight in the dream underwater world they discover; those who prefer exploring the sea from above the waterline can go on a whale and dolphin safari tour

The Magazine

these creatures. Boat trips are available both from the harbour in Corralejo and from Caleta de Fuste. The latter is where the Oceanarium Explorer catamaran is based, which offers trips several times a weeks. They claim to spot dolphin and whales (on average) on 40 per cent of trips, and sea turtles on 95 per cent of trips.

Diving

All operators offer beginner's courses and cater for experienced divers. Angel sharks and rays are the top sights. Recommended operators are Corralejo Dive Centre (tel: 928 535 906; www.divecentrecorralejo.com) and Punta Amanay Dive Centre (tel: 928 535 357; www.punta-amanay.com). The Corralejo Dive Centre is the longest-established on the island, with more than 30 dive sites. A good diving base on the east coast is Deep Blue (tel: 928 163 712; www.deep-blue-diving.com) in Caleta de Fuste; another is Acuarios Jandía (tel: 928 876 069; www.acuarios-jandia.com), which is based in Costa Calma in the Sotavento Beach Club.

The minimum age for diving is usually 10 or 12 years old.

Snorkelling safaris and diving trips promise an unforgettable experience in the underwater world

Snorkelling safaris

You can go on a "snorkelling safari" with Get Wet in Corralejo (www.getwet-snorkelling-fuerteventura.com, tel: 660 77 80 53). On these excursions there is a good chance you will spot dolphins, turtles and rays. After a fun high-speed boat ride to the dive site in an inflatable, you don a wetsuit and follow a guide to places where marine life is regularly sighted. Get Wet visits Isla de Lobos. Trips last between two and four hours in total with around an hour actually snorkelling. Children over 8 years of age can also take part in snorkel safaris. Glass-bottom boats go from Corralejo to the Isla de Lobos (►48), and you can also do "submarine boat" trips from Caleta de Fuste and Morro Jable.

SHIPWRECKS

The crashing waves and high winds which fuel the island's extreme water sports can mean disaster for commercial shipping, and over the last two decades Fuerteventura has seen many wrecks. Fortunately, only a few lives have been lost and wrecks that have happened close to shore have become sightseeing attractions.

In 1987, the *Rose of Sharon*, a 37m (121ft) two-masted wooden schooner, built in 1936, washed up on the sands of Jandía and remained there for several years, becoming the archetypal desert island shipwreck. It became an unofficial island symbol, even appearing on the front cover of tourist brochures. In 1995 the somewhat less picturesque 100m (328ft) container ship *Jucar* broke up on the shore of Aguas Verdes. In 1999 the *FV Massira*, a deep-sea fishing vessel, went ashore north of El Cotillo and became a popular tourist attraction.

The biggest and most spectacular wreck of all was the *SS American Star*, which between 1993 and 2007 reigned supreme as the island's

A painting of the *SS American Star*

The Magazine

unofficial number one sight. On a darker note, many boats packed with illegal immigrants from West Africa have recently been dashed on the rocks with many fatalities. And accidents continue to happen, even close to shore. In 2007 an environmental protection vessel went to Davy Jones' Locker in Corralejo harbour – fortunately there were no deaths.

SS American Star

Launched in 1939 as a luxury cruise liner capable of carrying more than 1,200 passengers, and measuring a mighty 220m (723ft) by 28m (93ft), the ship spent the war on troop-carrying duty, then resumed transatlantic cruises until 1963 when she began a new life carrying emigrants from the UK to Australia. In 1993 she was sold off, to be towed to Thailand and used as a floating hotel. The shortest and easiest route was via the Suez Canal. However, it appears her owners chose not to pay the Canal fees and instead made the fatal decision to go along the African coast during storm season. She beached some 100m off the west coast of Fuerteventura at Playa de Garcey and soon split in two.

Within days of the wreck occurring it is said that half the island's inhabitants had paid her a visit and taken away a "souvenir", though none went so far as the owners of the **Café El Naufragio** who "salvaged" whole cabin sections which can now been seen in Puerto del Rosario (▶75). While there were no deaths as a direct result of the shipwreck there were eight subsequent fatalities, including a man who attempted to swim out to the wreck and was apparently drawn into the chasm at the break; two treasure seekers met a tragic end when the section they were exploring collapsed beneath them, and another poor soul ended his life by jumping into the sea from the bow section.

Salvaged ship cabins and signs can be seen at Café El Naufragio in Puerto del Rosario

The Magazine

My Fuerteventura

Fuerteventura has a laid-back lifestyle all its own. Two "foreigners" who run very successful tourist businesses here give their views, along with a true *majorero*, whose mission is to preserve his island's identity.

Animal magic

Five years ago Maria Lazaga Romero was a successful lawyer in her hometown of Las Palmas, but gave it up to manage La Lajita Oasis Park (▶93) in the backwoods of Fuerteventura. During Maria's four years as general manager the park has become one of the biggest tourist attractions in the Canaries. Maria's colleagues constantly interrupt us but she insists, "here, when I leave work I have no stress. I walk and swim at Tarajalejo or Risco El Paso, you see only the birds and sea."

Surf's up

Also born in Gran Canaria but with his formative years spent in Cornwall, Ben Thomas (photo) moved to Fuerteventura in 1985 and is the owner of Flag Beach Windsurf and Kitesurf Centre, the biggest water sports operator in the north of the island (▶64). Today, Ben employs up to nine people in his international, multilingual team.

My Land, my Country

Tinín Martínez is president of the environmental group Mahoh, which means "my land/my country". The movement came into being at the beginning of the 1980s as a response to proposed building on the sand dunes of Corralejo. After much campaigning by Mahoh, the dunes were declared a national park. Since then, 13 other areas of the island have also been declared National Protected Spaces. "Twenty years ago I did not oppose development, as long as it was sensitive development," recalls Tinín, "but today I am campaigning for a full stop until we have caught up with what is currently underway. We must learn the mistakes of the coast and conserve the interior".

Both locals and foreigners have found success in tourism

Finding Your Feet

First Two Hours	36
Getting Around	37
Accommodation	38
Food and Drink	39
Shopping	41
Entertainment	42

Finding Your Feet

First Two Hours

Arriving by air
- The **Aeropuerto de Fuerteventura** is 5km (3mi) south of Puerto del Rosario on the east coast, tel: 928 860 500; www.aena.es.
- The major **car hire** companies have desks in the Arrivals Hall.
- There are currency exchange facilities, a café and basic shops, including a bookshop where you can buy island maps.

Getting to your resort from the airport
- **Taxis** are the quickest but most expensive option and leave from outside the airport building. Official prices are posted by the luggage carousel, at the airport information desk. Airport Taxis tel: 928 855 432.
- There is a direct **bus** service from the airport, just outside the terminal building, to Caleta de Fuste (No 3), Costa Calma (No 10) and Morro Jable (No 10). If you are staying in Corralejo or El Cotillo catch No 1 or 3 to Puerto del Rosario then take bus No 6 to Corralejo or No 7 to El Cotillo. (Bus No 8 links Corralejo to El Cotillo.)

Car hire at the airport
- Several major car hire companies have offices at the **airport**. Car hire is also **widely available** in the **main resorts** so unless you are staying somewhere remote you may have the option of travelling to your accommodation by bus or taxi then hiring a car when you get there (see opposite for more on car hire).

Arriving/Departing by sea

Tenerife and Gran Canaria
- **Passenger and car ferries** from Puerto del Rosario to Gran Canaria (Las Palmas), Morro Jable to Las Palmas, Morro Jable to Santa Cruz de Tenerife, Corralejo to Playa Blanca (Lanzarote), and Gran Tarajal/Puerto del Rosario to Las Palmas are operated by Naviera Armas shipping line (tel: 902 456 500; www.naviera-armas.com).

Lanzarote
- Passengers from Lanzarote (either Playa Blanca or Puerto del Carmen) arrive at Corralejo.
- Fred Olsen (tel: 902 100 107; www.fredolsen.es) and Naviera Armas (tel: 902 456 500) run a daily service every two hours from 7am (first boat from Playa Blanca) to 8pm (last return to Playa Blanca).

Tourist Information Offices
- Most tourist office staff speak English and can issue **maps and information** in English.

Airport
- There is an office in the **Arrivals Hall**. Open: Mon–Sat 9–8, Sun 10–5 in winter, and Mon–Sat 9–7, Sun 11–4 in summer (tel: 928 860 604).

Resorts
- **Corralejo**. Playa Muelle Chico, Avenida Marítima 2. Open: Mon–Fri 8–3, Sat, Sun 9–3; 8–2 Jul, Aug and Sep (tel: 928 866 235; www.corralejo

Getting Around

grandesplayas.com). **Caleta de Fuste**, CC Castillo Centro, Calle Juan Ramón Soto Morales. Open: Mon–Fri 9–2 (tel: 928 163 611). **Jandía Playa/Morro Jable**. CC Cosmo Local 88. Open: Mon–Fri 8–3 (tel: 928 540 776). Morro Jable, on the beach just off the promenade there are three kiosks. One is open 10–1 and two are open 10–5.

- The **Patronato Insular de Turismo** (Island Tourist Board) has its offices at Almirante Lallermand, 1 in Puerto del Rosario. Open: Mon–Fri 8–3; 8–2 Jun–Sep (tel: 928 530 844).
- There are also tourist information kiosks at: **Antigua** Main square. Open: Mon–Fri 10–2 (tel: 928 163 286). **Betancuria**, next to the church. Open: Mon–Fri 10–2:30. **Gran Tarajal**, Avenida Paco Hierro, just off the main promenade. Open: Mon–Fri 10–2:30, Sat 9–1 (tel: 928 162 723).

Getting Around

Buses
- Buses are operated by **Tiadhe** (tel: 928 855 726; www.maxoratabus.com) and are modern and comfortable. However, the service between resorts and places of interest is infrequent. Pick up a timetable from the nearest bus station or tourist office, or go online.

Taxis
- Taxis are usually white and have a green light on the top which when illuminated indicates that they are available for hire.
- For **local** journeys, fares are **metered** (53–60¢ per km, min €3.05 (daytime), €3.35 (evening), but if travelling across municipal boundaries the meter does not apply and you must **agree a fare** in advance.
- Use the **regulated list of taxi fares** at the airport (see opposite) as a guide.
- You can usually hail a taxi on the street. The resorts and Puerto del Rosario have taxi ranks but at night book through your hotel.
- Taxi telephone numbers: Corralejo: 928 866 108, Morro Jable 928 541 257

Driving
- If you want to explore, you need to hire a car (see below). On the whole driving is enjoyable with very **little traffic** and well-surfaced roads. The only downside is that this encourages **fast driving** so be wary of your own speed and that of the locals.
- **Take great care** when pulling off the road as the surface is nearly always raised 20cm (8in) or so above the ground level and you could easily damage the underneath of your vehicle. *Miradores* (lookout points) are usually provided in the mountains at particularly scenic spots so that you can pull over safely to enjoy the view.

Car hire
- Most **major international** car hire companies have offices at the airport.
- **Local companies** usually offer the best deals. If you want the security of a pre-booked car, however, you can use the services of a broker such as

Insider Tip

Finding Your Feet

Holiday Autos (UK tel: 0870 400 4461) or visit www.holidayautos.co.uk or www.holidayautos.de.

- To **hire a car** you will need your passport, driver's licence and credit card. Keep these papers on you at all times, along with the car hire documents.
- If you intend driving off road, hire a **4WD/jeep** that the car hire company recommends for this purpose. These are available from all the main operators but book as far in advance as possible as they only have limited numbers.
  If you have an accident or damage the underside of any other vehicle while driving off road, your **insurance** will not cover this. Note that some operators threaten to levy a fine of around €120 (to cover the cost of wear and tear) if they see drivers take their ordinary saloon cars off road. You may wish to ask about this at time of hire or consult the small print in your contract.
- It's usually worth paying that bit extra for **air conditioning**.

Driving essentials
- Drive on the **right-hand** side of the road.
- **Seat belts** are compulsory for the driver and all passengers.
- The legal **alcohol** limit is 50mg alcohol per 100ml blood and for new drivers (= holder of a driving licence for less than two years) 30mg.
- **Speed limits** are 90kph (56mph) on the open road and 40kph (25mph) in urban areas unless otherwise indicated.
- Use your **horn** on blind bends in the mountains.
- **Fuel** is much cheaper than in northern Europe and on mainland Spain. Filling stations are few and far between in the mountains, so keep your tank topped up. Most, but not all, accept credit cards.
- **Theft** from cars is not a problem; nonetheless, lock valuable items in the boot.
- **Beware** that almost every town and village, no matter how small, has a one-way system. Be careful as they are not always well signposted – if every car in the street is parked facing towards you, you are probably going the wrong way!
- **Blue lines** indicate pay-and-display metered parking areas, yellow lines mean no parking.

Accommodation

The majority of hotels and apartments are booked by tour operators so independent travellers may experience some difficulty in finding places to stay. However, there is usually a surfeit of accommodation on the island so even in high season and holiday times there is always still a reasonable chance of getting something reasonable on spec.

- **Timeshare** touts do exist on Fuerteventura but are not yet a major problem. However, with the amount of new construction in the pipeline they are likely to increase in numbers. Be wary of anyone stopping you in the street or offering free excursions or prizes, as hard-sell tactics are often used to get your signature on a property deal. The golden rule is sign nothing without consulting your lawyer.

Food and Drink

Hotels
- All hotels are officially **graded from 1 to 5 stars**, with most establishments rated as 3 stars or higher. In this category all bedrooms have a private bathroom.
- The hotels and apartments on the following pages have been selected because of their quality, special character or as being good value within their class or price range. Accommodation is more expensive during the **peak season** (late October to April). There is a **second peak** in late July and August when many Spanish families as well as northern Europeans are on holiday. The quietest months are May, June, early July, September and early October.

Apartments
- Apartments are **graded from 1 to 3 keys**, and even the simplest has a bedroom, bathroom, lounge, kitchenette and balcony. Bed linen, bath towels and maid service are usually included in the price; equipment such as TVs, kettles and toasters can usually be hired for an extra charge. Aparthotels are large apartment blocks with all the facilities of a hotel, such as a swimming pool, restaurant and evening entertainment.
- The majority of **self-catering accommodation** is pre-booked by package tourists but if you ask around in a resort you can usually find an apartment to let.

Casas rurales
- *Casa rurales* are village houses and farmsteads that have been converted into holiday cottages for rent. They are all small (accommodating a maximum of six people) and all are outside the resorts so you will definitely need a car. They are decorated in a rustic style (bare stone or wooden floors and rag rugs) and offer very good value, though not all have mod cons, and certainly no air conditioning! If you crave a little more comfort, choose one of the island's three **hoteles rurales**, which accommodate more people, albeit still on a very small scale, and offer more facilities (www.ecoturismocanarias.com). [Insider Tip]

Prices

The symbols refer to the average cost of a double room or one-bedroom apartment in high season. In the case of larger hotels these are published "rack rates" and can usually be negotiated down.

€ under €60   €€ €60–90   €€€ €91–120   €€€€ over €120

Food and Drink

Most restaurants in Fuerteventura offer Canarian cuisine (➤ 22) together with steaks, seafood dishes and traditional Spanish favourites. Fresh fish is available all over the island.

What and where to eat
- Resorts such as Corralejo, Morro Jable, Jandía Playa and particularly Caleta de Fuste have a **full range of restaurants** offering English

Finding Your Feet

breakfasts, hamburgers, pizzas, *Wiener Schnitzel*, and other reminders of home, to their international clients.
- Many bars and some restaurants offer **tapas**, small portions of Spanish and Canarian food, which can either be starters, snacks or combined to act as a full meal.

> **Popular tapas (➤ 22)**
> *Albóndigas* – meatballs
> *Croquetas* – croquettes, which may be filled with potato or seafood
> *Gambas* – shrimps
> *Pimientos* – peppers, which may be stuffed with a variety of fillings so enquire
> *Pulpo* – octopus
> *Tortilla* – potato omelette
> *Champiñónes* – mushrooms usually stuffed with garlic and fried

Eating out – a practical guide

- The traditional **mealtimes** are 1–4 for lunch and 8–11 for dinner, though many restaurants are open throughout the day to cater for the varying demands of locals and tourists.
- Some restaurants offer a fixed-price ***menú del día***, though this is the exception rather than the rule and is more likely to appear at lunchtime.
- By law, **service** is included in the price, though there may be a nominal cover charge for items such as bread and olives or other snacks, which appear on the table unrequested. If you are happy with the service (see below) leave a tip of between five and ten per cent. In bars leave some small change on the counter.
- Service is variable. Particularly in some local bars, standards of service may appear low (even unacceptably rude) to north Europeans while this is accepted as the norm locally.
- **Booking** is rarely necessary except at the smartest or most popular restaurants (noted in the guide under regions). However, to avoid disappointment it may be worth making a reservation for Saturday dinner or Sunday lunch.
- **Prices**: With just a few exceptions, there is surprisingly little difference in prices when eating out. It is quite acceptable to order two starters and no main course, or a single starter for two people to share.
- **Insider Tip** "Children's menu" generally means fast food or international food. If you want to avoid this, just ask for a smaller portion *(porción pequeña)* of an adult dish.

A guide to drinking

- **Mineral water** is available everywhere. Ask for *agua sin gas* (still) or *agua con gas* (sparkling).
- **Coffee** is served as *café solo* (a small shot of strong black coffee, like an espresso) or *café con leche* (with milk). The latter is usually served with steamed milk and is similar to a cappuccino though some places may simply add warm, or even cold, milk. If you want an instant coffee, ask for a nescafé. A *baraquillo* is a shot of brandy in a black coffee and is popular after dinner.
- Small quantities of **wine** are produced in Fuerteventura though the most common Canary island wine in Fuerteventura is malvasia, either dry or

Shopping

sweet, from Lanzarote. Good-quality wines are imported from all over the Spanish mainland.
- The **local spirit** is *ron* (rum) and *ronmiel* (literally honey rum) is a popular liqueur.
- Many restaurants routinely serve a complimentary glass of sweet local liqueur at the end of a meal.

> **Prices**
> The symbols indicate what you should pay per person for a three-course meal, excluding drinks and service charge.
> € under €15   €€ €15–25   €€€ over €25

Shopping

Despite Spain's membership of the European Union (EU), the Canary Islands have retained their special status as a free trade zone, with minimal import duties and a low rate of IGIC (Impuesto General Indirecto Canario), a general tax on sales, similar to VAT in the UK – although increases are planned. Many everyday and gift items, most notably alcohol, tobacco, perfume, jewellery and electronic goods, are considerably cheaper here than in many parts of mainland Europe.

Customs

Since the Canary Islands enjoy a special status, there are strict limits on the amount of goods that can be exported for personal use. The allowances to other EU countries are one litre of spirits, two litres of wine and either 200 cigarettes or 50 cigars.

Shopping areas

- The biggest **range** of shops is to be found in Corralejo and Jandía Playa, but still choice is limited. As well as Canarian crafts (see below), there are dozens of surf shops (usually very expensive); perfumeries and jewellers both offering duty-free prices; and electronics shops selling watches, cameras and high-tech goods. The latter are invariably run by Asian traders and prices are almost always negotiable.

Opening times

- Most shops are open Monday to Saturday from around 9:30/10–1:30 and 4:30/5–8. In Corralejo and Jandía Playa many shops open later, until around 10pm.
- The airport departure lounge has a surprisingly good choice of shops and good quality merchandise.

Canarian classics

- There are government-approved **artesanías** (craft shops) at Betancuria, El Molino de Antigua, the Ecomuseo de la Alcogida and at the airport. Everything on sale is handmade and there are no bargains.
- Locally produced goods include **basketry**, **embroidered lace**, **pottery** and **aloe vera** products.

Finding Your Feet

Insider Tip
- **Favourite foods** include *mojo* sauces, cheese and Canarian wines (usually from Lanzarote), Cuban-style cigars from La Palma.

Markets
- A general market for visitors tours the island every week (9–1, Corralejo Mon, Fri, Caleta de Fuste Sat, Jandía Playa Thur). Goods on sale include **leatherwork, clothes, linens, lace, embroidery** and **ceramics**. Be prepared for a little bartering to get a decent price. The market is held from 9–1 at Corralejo on Monday and Friday, Caleta de Fuste on Saturday and Jandía Playa on Thursday.

Five gifts made in Fuerteventura
- A Fuerteventura goat logo shirt/bag/other accessory
- A T-shirt with the island's famous podomorph (stylized footstep)
- Aloe vera products (but check they really are from Fuerteventura!)
- Handmade ethnic pottery
- A *pintadera* (see above)

Entertainment

Carnival and church festivals are celebrated in a big way on the island. Its nightlife tends to be focused around the tourist centres. And action and fun can also be found in the sports activities.

Festivals and folklore
- **Fiestas** on the island are not as big or frequent as on the other popular Canary Islands but they still celebrate **Carnival** (➤ 19), with the most colourful revelries in Corralejo and Puerto del Rosario.

Bars and clubs
- The busiest tourist **nightlife** is in Corralejo with the "music square" being the liveliest. Corralejo also has three good-quality nightspots. Caleta de Fuste and Jandía Playa also have a number of music bars. Locals will tell you that Puerto del Rosario has the best **nightclubs** on the island.

Sports
- Conditions for **water sports**, particularly **windsurfing** and **kiteboarding**, are among the best in the world (➤ 16).
- **Surfing** is also very popular particularly around Corralejo and El Cotillo (➤ 17).
- **Scuba-diving** is a popular activity with many accredited schools (➤ 31).
- Caleta de Fuste has two 18-hole **golf courses** complete with a golf hotel; there is a third 18-hole course in Las Playitas.

The North

Getting Your Bearings	44
The Perfect Day	46
TOP 10	48
At Your Leisure	55
Where to…	58

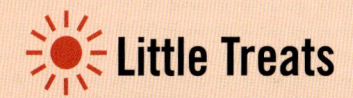

☀ Little Treats

Beautiful prospects
From the **lookout platform of Faro de Tostón** north of El Cotillo (➤ 55), you have a clear view to Lanzarote.

Little walk
On the road between Tindaya (➤ 57) and La Matilla a marked path leads up to **Fuente del Risco**.

Colonial roof terrace
In **La Oliva** you must go up on to the roof of the Casa de los Coroneles (➤ 53).

The North

Getting Your Bearings

Fuerteventura is often described as "a chip off the Sahara", with the coast of Africa just 100km (60mi) north west of Corralejo. And as you gaze out over the blinding dunes of Corralejo it seems a very apt description. Drive a little way inland and soft white sands change to jagged black rocks – malpais (volcanic debris) spilled from the dozens of volcanoes that were active here as recently as 8,000 years ago.

The island's only waymarked trail takes you on a lonely walk right into the heart of these "badlands", yet the north is also the busiest part of the island. All things are relative of course, and the biggest resort on Fuerteventura would hardly register a blip in Tenerife or Gran Canaria. However, if you have come to the island for peace and quiet, Corralejo should not be your first choice. It has wonderful beaches, a tremendous choice of places to eat, drink and make merry but while the old part retains its fishing village atmosphere, the new "strip" is modern and noisy.

For a taste of desert island bliss, slip quietly over to the Isla de Lobos. The unspoiled villages of Lajares and Villaverde are perfect country retreats and El Cotillo, with wonderful beaches for all activities and ages, has a rustic, half-forgotten air, though major new developments may change all that. La Oliva is a quiet administrative centre with some intriguing historical and art attractions, while to the south Montaña Tindaya, the sacred mountain of the Guanches, provides a taster of the island's inland delights.

Beach day on the Isla de Lobos

Getting Your Bearings

TOP 10
★ Isla de Lobos ➤ 48
★ Corralejo ➤ 50
★ La Oliva ➤ 53

At Your Leisure
11 El Cotillo ➤ 55
12 Lajares ➤ 56
13 Villaverde ➤ 56
14 Montaña Tindaya ➤ 57

Perfect Days in...

The North

Four Perfect Days

This suggested itinerary offers a good way to visit some of the most interesting sights in the north of Fuerteventura in just four days. For more information see the main entries (➤ 48–57).

Day One

Morning
Head out to the dunes of ⭐**Corralejo** (➤ 50) to see one of the island's natural wonders. Cross the road and spend the morning at Flag Beach, indulge yourself with some water sports at **Flag Beach Centre** (➤ 18) and either have a snack lunch at the beach bar here or save yourself for lunch at Villaverde.

Afternoon
Drive to **13 Villaverde** (➤ 56) and take your pick between its two excellent country restaurants, El Horno and the Hotel Rural Mahoh. After the meal go underground at the **Cueva del Llanos** (➤ 56).

Day Two

Morning
Drive to ⭐**La Oliva** (➤ 53) and visit the **Centro de Arte Canario**. Leave your car by the museum, visit the church, the Casa de los Coroneles and the nearby **Casa del Capellán** (➤ 53). Return to your car and visit the tiny **Museo del Grano La Cilla** (➤ 54) just around the corner. Get back on the main road and drive to **11 El Cotillo** (➤ 55) for lunch at El Veril, Azzuro or Torino's beach bar (➤ 59–60).

46

Afternoon

Spend the afternoon on the family-friendly Lagos lagoon beaches or catch a wave at the magnificent wild beaches to the south of town. Visit the beautifully restored **Torre del Tostón** (➤55) overlooking the new port and watch the sunset here. Finish your day with a meal on the jetty of Puerto Viejo (➤55).

Day Three

Get down to the port at Corralejo early to watch the comings and goings (photo above), have breakfast at **La Olá café** (➤58), then catch the 10am ferry to visit the ☆**Isla de Lobos** (➤48) for a day of desert island exploring and/or sunbathing. Return at either 4pm or 6pm and spend the rest of the evening shopping, bar-hopping and dining in Corralejo.

Day Four

Morning

Strap on your walking shoes, drive to Lajares and explore the north's volcanic landscape by taking the **Sendero de Bayuyo** (➤142). Return to **12 Lajares** (➤56), browse at the craft stalls, and either have a simple lunch at **El Arco** (➤60) or head to El Cotillo (photo left) for lunch at El Veril or Azzuro (➤59).

Afternoon

If you can drag yourself away from El Cotillo's beaches, drive towards La Oliva then head south to see the magical **14 Montaña Tindaya** (➤57). From here it's a very pleasant drive along the FV10 through La Matilla and Tetir until you reach the outskirts of Puerto del Rosario. Follow the signs back to Corralejo, which is 33km (20mi) north.

47

The North

⭐ 4 Isla de Lobos

It seems everything on the Isla de Lobos qualifies itself by a diminutive; *las lagunitas*, the little lagoons; *los hornitos*, the little volcanoes; El Puertito, the (ramshackle) little port. We would add to that by saying that this is the best little day trip that you can make. The absence of tourist development means that you can see an almost pristine island in its original state.

Isla de Lobos measures 4.4km² (1.7mi²) and you can walk right around the perimeter in less than two hours. Our featured walk (➤ 138) of around three hours takes you to all the island's places of interest and is highly recommended. The island name, literally "island of wolves", is derived from a colony of seals *(lobos marineros)*, in fact monk seals, which once lived here but have long since disappeared. It is recorded that the explorer and conquistador Gadifer de la Salle (number two to Jean de Béthencourt, ➤ 13) dropped anchor here in 1402 and he and his men were only saved from starving by eating seal meat. Béthencourt built a hermitage on the island and in the following centuries Lobos was used as a pirate and slave-trading base. Today the only permanent residents are António, the ex-lighthouse keeper, now island restaurateur, his family and a few friends who inhabit the dilapidated little hamlet of El Puertito. The lighthouse still functions but is now fully automated.

Two boats run to Isla de Lobos, including a glass-bottomed catamaran

Getting here
There are three boats that run daily to the island from Corralejo. *Isla de Lobos* is the regular service departing at 10 and noon, returning at 12:15 and 4pm. The *Celia Cruz* glass-bottomed catamaran departs at 9:45am and returns at 2:20pm and 6pm (mobile: 646 531 068; www.

INSIDER INFO

Avoid visiting on very windy days. Hidden gem El Puertito springs surprisingly to life around lunchtime. The smell of fresh fish wafts from Antonio's rustic restaurant, the little bay in front of here is ideal for swimming and divers also turn up here.

Isla de Lobos

View of the island volcano from Playa de la Caleta. The beach is also good for children

fuerteventura. net/celiacruz; Oct–May 5:15pm). The *El Majorero* departs at 10 and noon and returns at 12:30pm and 4pm (tel: 616 986 982; www.navie anortour.es).

If you intend to walk, sunbathe and eat in the restaurant here, choose the *Celia Cruz* as it gives you more time. The *Celia Cruz* also offers a daily one-hour cruise around the island. Pick up a flyer from their kiosk on the quay at Corralejo for departure times.

Getting about

It couldn't be easier. Signposts show you the way as soon as you disembark. The island's only settlement, **El Puertito**, is a seven-minute walk to the right; the 🏖 **beautiful beach of Playa la Concha** (aka Playa de la Caleta) lies six minutes to the left. Walkers and explorers will be delighted to find that a waymarked trail goes right around the island, with the furthest point being the **Faro** (lighthouse) **de Lobos**, a 50-minute walk due north.

Insider Tip

TAKING A BREAK

If you intend to eat at the island restaurant you MUST make a reservation as soon as you land (▶ 140 for more details).

✚ 163 F5

Centro des Visitantes Isla de Lobos
✉ Muelle
🕐 Daily 10:30–3

The North

⭐5 Corralejo

The biggest resort on the island, Corralejo has a loyal following, particularly among British and German visitors. The town divides neatly into "old port" and "new resort" with the dividing line being the pedestrianised zone. Just beyond this zone is the original fishing harbour, now a busy port where the Lanzarote and Lobos ferries, big-game fishing yachts and sleek catamarans jostle for space alongside traditional fishing boats.

The old part of town, particularly around the pedestrianised zone, is a picturesque area of small alleys and squares, most of which lead onto the seafront promenade, which is lined with attractive restaurants and bars. The epicentre of nocturnal activities is "Music Square", a tiny quadrangle hemmed in by restaurants with waiters touting for trade and a small stage where musicians serenade diners. To find the most authentic Spanish and local bars and restaurants, and some quaint little shops, just go a block or two further on towards the port. On Calle La Ballena it's hard to go wrong.

The modern part of town lies to either side of Avenida Nuestra Señora del Carmen, aka "The Strip". The Avenida is not unattractive and has several shopping centres, but don't expect to buy your designer gear here. However, if you want amusement arcades, cheap shops and eateries, as well as several Irish bars, then you should be happy (and well oiled) here.

🎎 Baku Water Park
The north's main visitor attraction began life as a water park with eight flumes and slides. It has now grown to

Corralejo is one of the largest tourist centres on the island, as is reflected in the wide choice of restaurants and bars

There are plenty of interesting sights, including the modern architecture

include two other major attractions – Animal Experience, with a petting zoo, sea lion and parrot shows (visitors can enter the water with the sea lions at an extra charge if they book in advance), and **El Hotel del Terror**, a haunted house with real actors. Other family-oriented activities include an enchanted castle, a zipwire, paintballing, a rock-climbing wall, mini-golf, ten-pin bowling and bingo. There is a Brazilian restaurant with shows every Friday evening and a market is held every Monday and Friday morning with African and Canarian handicrafts.

Beaches

The town harbour beach is the easy option, right in the centre, although it can get crowded. It is also not always as clean as one might wish. Look out for some very artistic and sophisticated sand sculptures here and do throw a coin or two in the artist's hat, particularly if you take a photograph. Moving east from the harbour a narrow beach runs almost all the way along the front. Playa Galera, in front of the Corralejo Beach hotel, is a nice stretch.

The best beaches lie 500m or so east of here and stretch for around 7km (4mi). You can easily walk from the newer part of town but if you are staying near the

INSIDER INFO

- If you are around during the second weekend in October, don't miss the **Kite Festival** held by the dunes.
- On the Avenida Fuerteventura (the main road to the beaches and dunes) keep your eyes peeled for the **Villa Tabaiba Galeria de Arte** (it's No 139 next to an apartment complex with an Irish pub). It is privately owned and open at irregular times (afternoons are the best bet), but even if there's no admission it's well worth stopping to peer into the garden to view the owner's eccentric collection of artworks heavily influenced by Salvador Dalí and Joan Miró.

Insider Tip

51

Escape to the dunes of the pristine Parque Natural de las Dunas de Corralejo

port and/or you are driving, then it is "just around the corner" from the main road into Corralejo (like most Spanish towns it has an unforgiving one-way system!).

Flag Beach is the main section and the next stretch along, by the two large Riu hotels, is known as **Glass Beach**. Windsurfers and kitesurfers will head to Flag Beach or Glass Beach but there are excellent surfing "beaches" (with no sand) heading west from the Bristol Playas apartments. Whichever beach you choose, directly across the water you will enjoy great views of Isla de Lobos and Lanzarote.

Parque Natural de las Dunas de Corralejo

Corralejo's white sand dunes cover an area of around 27km² (10mi²). This area was declared a national park in 1982, too late to stop the two hotels that were already built, but it did prevent further attempts to exploit this otherwise pristine natural landscape. Walk for ten minutes off the road, out of sight and sound of traffic and hotels, and you could imagine yourself in a Lawrence of Arabia world. The only creatures you will meet are a handful of goats and the occasional naturist.

TAKING A BREAK

If you're after a coffee or food, the **Antiguo Café del Puerto** (➤ 58) is an all-day option.

✚ 163 E5

Baku Water Park
✉ Avenida Nuestra Señora del Carmen
☎ 928 867 227; www.bakufuerteventura.com
🕐 Daily 10–5 (later in season)
💶 €25

⭐ La Oliva

Despite being the administrative centre of the north, La Oliva is no more than a large village and often has the appearance of a ghost town. Nonetheless, it has an interesting history and a number of unusual sights.

La Oliva has always been a seat of power on Fuerteventura. The Guanche king Guize (➤ 14) once ruled his northern territory from here, and after the conquest it was one of the first towns to be settled by the Europeans.

The Iglesia de Nuestra Señora de la Candelaria, built in 1711, has three naves, but its most striking feature is its black lava bell tower. Look inside to see its wine-glass-shaped pulpit and side altar decorated in matching patterns and its painting of Christ in Majesty (1732).

Casa de los Coroneles

In the 18th century, La Oliva was the seat of the military governor *(Los Coroneles)* and at times the de facto capital of Fuerteventura. These ruthless commanders ruled here until 1859, their official residence was the grandiose Casa de los Coroneles, a large castellated colonial-style house dating back to 1650. It is now one of the most historically interesting buildings on the island. It used to be said, quite erroneously, that there was a door and window for every day of the year and it is thought that the saying probably reflected the jealous unpopularity of the Colonel's regime.

The Nuestra Señora de la Candelaria church is well worth a visit

This came to an end in 1859 and thereafter the famous old house began a long slow decline into dereliction. After decades of promises of renewal had come and gone, restoration was completed and the Casa de Coroneles reopened in 2006 as an art gallery and cultural centre (open Tue–Sat 10–6; €3).

Centro de Arte Canario (CAC)

This cool contemporary space devoted to Canarian art, complete with soothing ambient New Age music, has wide-ranging appeal. The entrance is via a large sculpture and **cactus garden** with several interesting and witty pieces alluding to the island's flora, fauna and ancient history. Its centrepiece is the **Casa Mané**, a restored mid-19th-century house, including six paintings by Lanzarote guru César Manrique (➤ 108).

Art treasures in the Centro de Arte Canario

Museo del Grano La Cilla

A *cilla* is a storehouse for grain that belongs to the church, and this example dates from 1819. It was used to house wheat, barley, rye, pulses and some fruit. Today it is home to a small exhibition of photographs and agricultural implements that show how farming was done manually with the aid of donkeys and camels until the 1940s.

TAKING A BREAK

La Oliva is short of good cafés or restaurants but try **Hijos de Suarez** opposite the church (➤ 60).

✚ 163 D3

Centro de Arte Canario (CAC)
✉ Calle Salvador Manrique de Lara (opposite Casa de los Coroneles)
☎ 928 851 128; www.centrodeartecnario.com
🕒 Mon–Sat 10:30–2
💶 €4

Museo del Grano La Cilla
✉ Carretera El Cotillo
☎ 928 868 729
🕒 Currently closed

INSIDER INFO

- **Don't miss!** The village springs to life on 2 February for the four-day **fiesta of Nuestra Señora de la Candelaria**.
- The **Casa del Capellán** (House of the Chaplain) stands boarded up in a field of dilapidated smallholding buildings, around 100m to the right of the road that leads to the Casa de los Coroneles. Despite its run-down appearance, the fine carvings around the door of this modest single-storey 200-year-old house are reminiscent of the famous portal at the church at Pájara (➤ 78), often described as "Aztec" influenced.
- **Illuminate** the Iglesia de Nuestra Señora de la Candelaria by putting €1 in the slot.

At Your Leisure

11 El Cotillo

At first sight it might seem there's little to detain you here, but persevere and you'll find some of the most attractive beaches and some good fish restaurants (➤ 59) on the island. El Cotillo is also a great place to watch the sunset. Historical interest is provided by the restored **Fortaleza/Torre del Tostón** (Tostón Tower), constructed in 1740 to deter English, Moorish and Arab pirates. Today it is home to a tourist office – climb the stairs for fine views over the **Puerto Nuevo** (new harbour) with its little fishing boats sheltering behind a huge volcanic rock. The dramatic high-sided jet-black **Puerto Viejo** (old harbour), occupying the next cove along, is usually empty of boats.

Just south of the El Cotillo is the Playa del Castillo, one of Fuerteventura's most beautiful beaches. However, the big waves make it better for surfing than

> **THE POWER OF THE SEA**
> The restaurant El Veril in El Cotillo's old harbour features the work of island photographer Jo Hammer. Among his most powerful images are those of recent storms when the waves reached over 10m (32ft) high and gave El Cotillo a terrible battering. Postcard-sized prints are on sale and make a good souvenir.

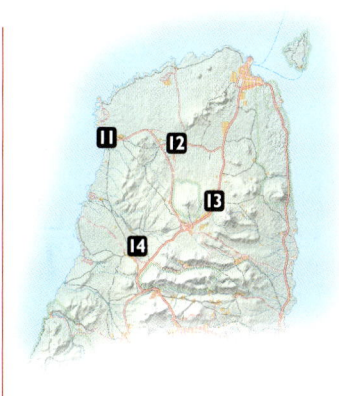

Fishing boats in the harbour of El Cotillo, in the background the Torre del Tostón

The North

swimming. The ⓘ **Playa de los Lagos** to the north is better for families.
➕ 162 C4

Torre del Tostón
✉ El Tostón

🔟 Lajares

This small roadside village has long been a popular stopping point for surfers en route to El Cotillo, and in recent years it has also attracted many foreign property buyers. The presence of both groups is reflected in a spate of good cafés, restaurants and surf shops. Lajares is also known for its long-established School of Embroidery, nowadays incorporated into an *artesanía* (handicrafts) shop (▶63). There are two fine examples of restored

> **THE CUEVA VILLAVERDE**
>
> The Cueva Villaverde is a cave formed by volcanic gases and lava, and measures some 190m long. It was used as a Guanche dwelling place and only discovered in 1979. There are long-term plans to open it up to the public but until then there is a small exhibition in the Centro Molino, La Antigua (▶83). Finds from the cave are on show in the Museo Arqueológico in Betancuria (▶72).

Lajares is famous for its school of embroidery. You can watch the intricate work that goes into lace-making

windmills near the church to the south of Lajares and the village is also the starting point for the Sendero de Bayuyo footpath (▶142).
➕ 163 D4

🔟 Villaverde

Villaverde is one of the best-preserved villages on the island. Perhaps the villagers are following the lead of the exemplary Hotel Rural Mahoh (▶60), which stands at the southern end of Villaverde and is worth a visit for its architecture and sculpture garden alone. The equally neat and tidy black-and-white stone farm buildings of **La Rosita** mark the northern entrance to the village. In the 1920s this was a tobacco and maize farm. A **cactus garden** surrounds the residence used until recently as an agricultural museum (currently closed).

From La Rosita head towards the centre of Villaverde and take the first turn right; after 300m is the ⓘ **Cueva del Llanos**. This cave is actually part of a much larger lava tube formed more than 690,000 years ago. The entrance to the cave is a part of the tube

Montaña Tindaya, the sacred mountain

where the roof has collapsed (known as a *jameo*) and contains a visitor centre with an exhibition, café and shop. From here visitors can walk along a lit pathway 400m into the cave which is some 7–10m (23–32ft) wide.

In 2014, the cave was closed because of flooding, so enquire when you get to Villaverde whether it is now possible to go inside again.
✚ 163 D3

Cueva del Llano
☎ 928 175 928 ⏰ Tue–Sat 10–6; tours every 45 minutes from 11–5 💶 €5

🔢 Montaña Tindaya
The original island dwellers regarded this mountain as sacred and came up here to worship their Supreme Deity, offering young goats as sacrifices. Their legacy is a number of inscriptions and rock carvings, only discovered as recently as 1978, on and around the summit of the mountain at 401m (1,315ft).

The most famous are over 100 feet-shaped carvings known as podomorphs. Most of them can only be made out with the help of a professional guide, but what you will find relatively easily on your own are the pairs of footprints about five metres below the summit near a big prickly pear cactus. They are thought to have been carved to keep away evil spirits. It takes just under two hours to reach the summit and on a clear day there are stunning views right across to Mount Teide. It is a strenuous climb, however, not suitable for inexperienced walkers and dangerous in wet or windy weather. Because of its sensitive nature you are required to have a permit, which in nearly all cases is issued on demand. Enquire at the Medio Ambiente (Environment Office) in Puerto del Rosario, Calle Lucha Canaria/Ecke Avenida Juan de Betancourt.
✚ 162 C3

The North

Where to...
Eat and Drink

Prices
Expect to pay for a three-course meal for one, excluding drinks and service
€ under €15   €€ €15–€25   €€€ over €25

CORRALEJO

Ambaradam €
Set on a quiet side street just off the top end of "The Strip", this Italian-owned and run café is a stylish, relaxed oasis in this part of town, perfect for a snack or full meal after visiting the market or the Baku amusement park. They specialise in breakfasts, sweet and savoury pancakes (no less than 47 kinds) and bruschetta (14 different types).
🕂 163 E5 ✉ Centro Commercial Cactus
☎ 696 996 207 🕐 Mon–Sat 8–1:30

Antiguo Café del Puerto €€ *(Insider Tip)*
This is the sort of place you will be welcome at any time of day or night, whether you want a *café con leche* (coffee with milk) or a beer while watching the boats on the seafront, or to make yourself a meal up from the good choice of tasty tapas in its attractive pastel-washed dining room. The staff are friendly and obliging.
🕂 163 E5 ✉ Calle La Ballena
☎ 928 537 024 🕐 Thu–Tue 11am–1am

Bodeguita El Andaluz €–€€
Manolo, the chef, is from Córdoba, and his menu is, like the restaurant itself, comprehensive but comfortingly small. After the tasty home-made bread and oil tuck into a starter of garlic prawns, or avocado, mozzarella and tomato, or perhaps baby lettuce with roasted garlic. A speciality from Córdoba is the rich gazpacho-like *salmorejo* soup. Meat dishes – superior quality steaks, chicken, pork fillet and kebab – come with a choice of green pepper, herb butter or creamy mushroom sauce, and there is always a fresh fish of the day. No credit cards taken.
🕂 163 E5 ✉ Calle La Ballena 5
☎ 676 705 878 🕐 Thu–Tue 7pm–11pm

Caracoles €€
Sylvia and Carlos are well known to Corralejo regulars for their authentic Spanish/Canarian cooking and serving up some of the best tapas to be found in town. An attractive little bar set in a narrow alleyway just off Music Square, it is unlikely to disappoint. Special offers such as six tapas and a bottle of wine for a set price makes the choosing less of a chore for confused visitors who would like a taste of everything.
🕂 163 E5 ✉ Just off Music Square
🕐 Tue–Sun 7–11pm (closed last Sun of month)

Factoria €–€€
Set right on the seafront, but just away from the main hubbub, this cheerful little pizzeria is one of the friendliest places in Corralejo. They do steaks and fish but specialise in pizzas (try something different such as the Felipin with broccoli, bacon and salmon). The perfect dining choice for young families.
🕂 163 E5 ✉ Avenida Marítima
☎ 928 535 726 🕐 Daily 10:30am–11pm

La Olá €
This attractive modern café attached to a bakery is just a

Where to...

stone's throw from the port. They do excellent breakfasts – try the *desayuno español* (Spanish breakfast), which includes toasted bread rubbed with tomato and topped with *jamón serrano* (cured ham). Despite being locals, they specialise in German pastries, cakes and cheesecake, and their iced coffee *frappé* is delicious.

The service is friendly and fast, and there are comfy cane chairs; sit inside or out.

🞤 163 E5
✉ Paseo Marítimo Bristol, Muelle Grande
☎ 928 535 304   🕐 Wed–Mon 7:30am–8pm

Taberna Fogalera €–€€

Open in the evenings, this seafront restaurant on the pedestrianised promenade serves Mediterranean cuisine, which besides Italian risotto and pasta also includes a good Spanish paella. Even the selection of wines is from Italy and Spain. There is a special 👶 children's menu: *"menù bambini"*.

🞤 163 E5 ✉ Avenida Marítima 12
☎ 928 867 676   🕐 Fri–Wed 6pm–11pm

Rogues Gallery €

The accent is firmly on rock and blues at this friendly British-run music bar. The volume always permits conversation, however, and there is no TV. Live music is performed by a guitarist every Saturday night.

🞤 163 E5 ✉ Calle La Ballena 3
🕐 Tue–Sun 10–1, 5–late

EL COTILLO

Aguayre €

This trendy modern bar overlooking the new port is the ideal place to catch the famous El Cotillo sunset with a beer, smoothie, milkshake or *chai latte* in your hand. There's even a couple of hammocks in which to chill out. Gourmet sandwiches and international snacks such as chilli and burritos are served throughout the day.

🞤 162 C4 ✉ Puerto Nuevo
🕐 Daily 9:30–9

Azzurro €€

In the detached house on the road to Faro del Tostón, the menu includes Italian dishes, a broad range of Canarian dishes and a good choice of vegetarian dishes. The paella and the *scoglio* (seafood) *tagliatelle* with mushrooms and prawns in a parmesan nest are highly recommended. Relax in the cosy traditional stone interior or on the terrace, watching the sunset alongside a mixed crowd of diners. There is live music every Friday at sunset. Azzurro provides excellent service and superb house wines.

🞤 162 C4
✉ Urb. Los Lagos 1, Carretera al Faro
☎ 928 175 360
🕐 Tue–Sun 12:30–10:30

El Goloso €

The French bakery on the northern edge of El Cotillo has a tempting selection of baguettes, croissants, country-style breads, various quiches, delicious fruit tartlets and other sweet pastries. You can buy everything to take away, but there are a few small tables for people who want to enjoy their breakfast and a good coffee in the bakery. In the main season, El Goloso is always busy.

🞤 162 C4
✉ Calle Pedro Cabrera Saavedra/
Calle León y Castillo   ☎ 928 53 86 68
🕐 7:30–2:30, 5–8, Sun in the morning only

Torino €–€€

This friendly little beach bar next to the lagoon beaches serves a good range of snacks and full meals and is the ideal place to eat with warm sand between your toes. The garlic prawns are wonderful and the paella is good, but give the cheese and tomato salad a miss.

🞤 162 C4 ✉ Playa Lagos
🕐 Daily 10–5

59

The North

El Veril €€
Unassuming from the front, the interior of this splendidly restored old house is one of the nicest places on the island to enjoy first-class Spanish and new wave Canarian cooking. The chef is Basque, and fish, meat and vegetarian dishes reflect the craft, style and top-class reputation of his home region. El Veril also has a large roof terrace overlooking the old harbour.

162 C4 ✉ Muelle de los Pescadores
☎ 928 538 780; www.restauranteelveril.com
🕐 Tue–Sat 6pm–midnight,
Sun 1–4, 7–midnight

LAJARES

El Arco €
This friendly and very well run roadside café is the perfect place for a simple sandwich or more substantial snack when you want to sit with the locals and ex-pats and eat without fuss. El Arco offers excellent value *bocadillos* – especially recommended is the *lomo especial* with pork, *alioli* (whisked oil and garlic), salad, egg and cheese – and *platos combinados* (combined dishes).

163 D4 ✉ Carretera Lajares–El Cotillo
☎ 928 868 071
🕐 Mon–Fri 9am–11pm, Sat 9–5

Canela €–€€
The plain tables and chairs on the pavement in front of the Canela and inside give this popular café/restaurant an air of no-frills simplicity. Located on the main street of Lajares, it is a favourite haunt of the younger crowd, who go there during the day to enjoy the colourful fusion cuisine of Asian curries, Arab Falafel, Greek salad and Mexican burritos. From 6pm, the kitchen extends its repertoire to include steaks.

163 D4
✉ Calle Coronel Gonzalez del Hiero 34 (Main road from Lajares–El Cotillo)
☎ 928 861 712 🕐 Daily 8am–2am

LA OLIVA

Hijos de Suarez €
Considering it is the administrative centre of the north, La Oliva's choice of restaurants is fairly modest. Opposite the parish church, you can buy simple meals, sandwiches *(bocadillos)* and freshly pressed juices and sit at one of the small tables on the pavement to eat them.

163 D3 ✉ Opposite the Iglesia Nuestra Señora de la Candelaria ☎ 928 868 679
🕐 Daily 10–7

VILLAVERDE

El Horno €€
The large barbecue at the entrance to this attractive rustic restaurant tells you that the speciality of the house is grilled meats. Start with aubergine with cheese and palm honey then perhaps *cochinillo* (suckling pig) or kid. Finish with fig or *gofio* ice cream. Lots of greenery and traditional Canarian music.

163 D3
✉ Carretera General Villaverde–La Oliva, 191
☎ 928 868 671, 629 382 304
🕐 Mon–Sat 12:30pm–11pm, Sun 12:30pm–10pm

Hotel Rural Mahoh €€ *Insider Tip*
Choose from one of the most interesting Canarian menus on the island while relaxing in one of its most charming settings. Start with delicious croquettes, stuffed peppers or baby squid with *mojo verde*; for mains try *vieja* (parrot fish) or goat, and finish with *leche frita* or fig ice cream smothered in mouthwatering warm chocolate sauce.

The daily *menú de la casa* (house special) is excellent value and on Sundays there are roast specials on the blackboard. It is a very romantic setting by night and there is always excellent service.

163 D3 ✉ Sitio de Juan Bello,
Carretera Villaverde–La Oliva
☎ 928 868 050; www.mahoh.com
🕐 Thu–Tue 1–11

Where to...
Stay

Prices
Expect to pay per double room, per night
€ under €60   €€ €60–€90   €€€ €91–€120   €€€€ over €120

Note that many of the larger hotels and apartments in Corralejo are block booked by big tour operators.

CORRALEJO

Atlantis Bahía Real €€€€
If your idea of a holiday is pampered luxury, then this 5-star 250-room grand hotel in Moorish-style right on the beachfront, just out of town, is ideal. All rooms enjoy magnificent sea views, there are three gourmet restaurants to eat your way through and the largest and best-equipped spa on the island, with a Turkish Bath, an ice fountain, a shower temple, a large open-air jacuzzi, a spinning room and just about any treatment you could wish for.
163 E5 ✉ Avenida Grandes Playas s/n
☎ 928 536 444; www.atlantisbahiareal.com

Brisamar €
The popular Brisamar aparthotel offers spacious and comfortable one- or two-bedroom apartments with a terrace at a very reasonable price. The hotel features saltwater swimming pools (including one for children), two tennis courts and a playground.
163 E5
✉ Avenida Nuestra Señora del Carmen
☎ 928 866 525;
www.apartamentosbrisamar.com

Corralejo Beach €
One of the town's original and favourite accommodations, the Corralejo Beach, fully renovated in 2007, enjoys a good beachfront location right in the centre of the resort. It includes 156 studios and apartments, with basic but functional furnishings, many with views towards Lanzarote and Isla de Lobos. Facilities include a sauna, solarium and a swimming pool. It also has its own disco pub.
163 E5 ✉ Calle Víctor Gra Bassas s/n
☎ 928 068 000; www.corralejobeach.com

Los Delfines €
This simple, white, two-storey apartment complex is rated 3-keys and is a five-minute walk from the beach. The apartments are attractively arranged around the pool area and each has its own terrace or balcony. Facilities include a buffet restaurant and squash courts.
163 E5
✉ Calle El Pozo 3 ☎ 928 535 153;
www.apartamentoslosdelfines.com

Hesperia Bristol Playa €€€
This attractive 3-keys aparthotel is situated on the seafront near the port and comprises 186 units in landscaped gardens. Apartments are well equipped and have a kitchen; facilities include three outdoor swimming pools, tennis courts and garden bar.
163 E5 ✉ Urbanización Lago de Bristol 1
☎ 928 867 020; www.hesperia-bristolplaya.com

La Posada €
This comfortable, modern three-storey 34-room hotel is set in the pedestrianised part of town just two minutes from the port.

The North

However, while it is quiet during the day, it is very noisy from 4pm to 8pm due to the large children's playground in front of it. The staff and owners are very friendly and obliging. Good breakfast. There's also a roof terrace. Excellent value.

✚ 163 E5 ✉ Calle María Santana Figueroa
☎ 928 867 344

Riu Palace Tres Islas €€€€
If location is your priority, the luxurious 4-star Tres Islas is one of the best options, located by magnificent white beaches right next to the dunes. It has two large swimming pools set in beautiful oasis-like grounds. The three isles referred to in the hotel's name are Lanzarote and Lobos (there are wonderful views of them just across the water) and Fuerteventura itself.

✚ 163 E5 ✉ Avenida Grandes Playas
☎ 928 535 700; www.riu.com

VILLAVERDE

Hotel Rural Mahoh €€
The Mahoh is an old country house built from volcanic stone and wood and dates from the 19th century. It has nine bedrooms with stone floors, all furnished with antiques, four of them with four-poster beds, and all exuding a rustic and romantic feel. Within its manicured grounds there is a swimming pool, a multi-purpose sports area with tennis and horse-riding stables. Its restaurant (▶60) is one of the best on the island so *media pensión* (half board) is recommended. Breakfast is included in the price.

✚ 163 D3 ✉ Sitio de Juan Bello, Carretera Villaverde-La Oliva
☎ 928 868 050; www.mahoh.com

EL COTILLO

Casa Tile €€
Set 2km (1mi) inland from El Cotillo this mid-19th-century country house is a perfect holiday hideaway for up to four people. The house has been in the same family for more than 150 years and has been recently sympathetically renovated and restored to retain its character. The living area, bathroom and bedrooms are separated from the kitchen and dining area by an open courtyard and there is a small (3m × 4m/10ft × 13ft) pool. Other facilities include a TV, washing machine and barbecue. Minimum stay during mid and high season is one week.

✚ 162 C4 ✉ El Roque
☎ 928 851 620; www.momentorural.com

Cotillo Sunset Apartments €–€€ *Ins Tip*
Right on the beach and a five-minute walk from the beautiful Lagos coves, this smart little modern complex comprises 32 two-storey studios. Each is attractively furnished and has well-equipped kitchens, including a microwave oven and toaster. All have a balcony/terrace with patio furniture. There is a 12m × 6m (40ft × 20ft) pool, a children's paddling pool and a heated outdoor jacuzzi.

✚ 162 C4 ✉ Avenida de los Dos Lagos
☎ 928 175 065

LAJARES

El Patio de Lajares €€€
This charming, stylish German-run "restaurant with rooms" is entered via a traditional-style patio and has six comfortable and spacious air-conditioned rooms in modern-traditional style and furnished to a high standard. Each has a terrace, satellite TV (English channels), mini bar, and a luxurious bathroom including bathrobes. There's a swimming pool, and wellness facilities include a Japanese foot bath, a small fitness centre and aloe vera treatments. The restaurant is highly recommended.

✚ 163 D4 ✉ Calle la Cerca 9, Lajares
☎ 650 134 030; www.patio-lajares.com

Where to... Shop

Shopping in the north of the island is concentrated on the *centros comerciales* (shopping centres) and main street of Corralejo. There are very few shops elsewhere in this region.

CORRALEJO

The resort's "high street", Avenida Nuestra Señora del Carmen, and the many shopping centres that lead off here feature scores of fashion clothes shops. Surf wear is predominant. International retail names sell at similar prices to northern Europe.

Anyone looking for original Italian female fashion should go to **Las Gatas** with its Gaudí-like entrance.

Another unusual shop is the **Panadería de Don Juan** at number 20. This old-fashioned, long-established bakery is ideal if you're self catering, and they have a small café attached too.

Cool T-Shirts and accessories bearing the goat skeleton logo of Extreme Animals are available in the **Calle Las Dunas**.

If you are after the ethnic look, Indian jewellery and Thai silver, then rummage through the **Isis Boutique – Aladdin's Cave** (Calle La Iglesia 3).

The **Herbolario Pachamama** has a large selection of organic food and natural cosmetics (Calle Francisco Navarro Artiles 2).

There are some pleasant little individual outlets dotted around the harbour. **Mystic**, on the corner of Calle María Santana Figueroa and Calle Isla de Lobos, is probably the best of Corralejo's many "world shops". They feature aloe vera products, Haitian art, some intriguing large wooden sculptures and objets d'art, stylish silk clothes, ethnic jewellery and accessories.

Corralejo's **market** (►42) takes place every Monday and Friday 9am to 1pm at Baku on Avenida Nuestra Señora del Carmen and is a good place to go if you enjoy African-style goods.

VILLAVERDE

The Casa Marcos, on the main road, is geared up for coach parties and resembles a mini-village. It has a good range of wines, cheeses, preserves, pottery and souvenirs.

LA OLIVA

The Centro de Arte Canario sells a wide range of works by local artists, from inexpensive postcards to expensive originals.

LAJARES

Lajares is famous for its embroidery school, which is now part of one of the island's best *artesanías* (craft shops). You'll find it on the main road in the centre of the village. Founded in 1950, it claims to be the only original Canarian embroidery workshop on the island and is famous for its openwork embroidery tablecloths and serviettes as well as lace items.

The **Artesanía Lajares** also sells a wide range of other handicrafts, plus aloe vera products, clothing, food, wine, cheese and preserves.

Surfers regularly pass through Lajares en route to neighbouring El Cotillo and there are a handful of specialist surfing shops. If you need a board, suit or just a t-shirt then **Witchcraft** and **North Shore** at either end of the village have some funky gear.

The Centre

Where to... Go Out

The beaches of Corralejo and El Cotillo are famous for their excellent water sports conditions (▶16). Corralejo is also a lively town after dark – the action is largely dispersed among its many disco and karaoke bars, sports bars and British-style pubs, although there are no "significant" nightclubs.

WATER SPORTS

For the best windsurfing and kiteboarding (▶16), go to the Playas de Corralejo and Playa Castillo at El Cotillo. **Flag Beach Windsurf and Kitesurf Centre** (tel: 928 866 389; 630 062 131, UK 0871 711 5036: www.flagbeach.com) is the north's biggest and longest-established water sports operator. It is located on Flag Beach (just look for the name in big letters on its hut, clearly visible from the main road). First-class, highly structured, friendly tuition from beginners to advanced level is available in windsurfing, surfing, bodyboarding and kitesurfing. This is the only centre where you can have a go at all these sports. Surfers will also catch a wave at El Cotillo and at the beaches west of Corralejo harbour. For diving schools, ▶31.

NIGHTLIFE

Corralejo bars and pubs play host to a lively music scene. One of the best is the **Rock Island Bar** (www.rockislandbar.com) at Calle Crucero Baleares, with live acoustic acts every evening. **Imagine** (Calle Lepanto, www.imaginemusicbar.com) is another bar dedicated to high quality live acoustic music, open nightly. Irish bands and local musicians play live nightly at **Rosie O'Grady's** on Calle Pizarro and at **The Dubliner** in the CC Atlántico. Every evening on the plaza surrounded by terrace cafés in the old town centre, a band plays Evergreen and Spanish music.

If you're looking for a disco try the **Waikiki** (waikikibeachclub.es) at Avenida Hernández Morán 11.

During the day, the **Beach Club** on the beach has a bistro-like atmosphere, which chills even further in the evening with tropical cocktails and good music.

If tongue-in-cheek cross-dressing is your scene then **Sadie's Drag Bar** on Calle Isaac Peral provides a night of comedy and cabaret (Thu–Tue 8pm–2am).

EXCURSIONS

By Boat
A day aboard the *Catlanza* (tel: 928 513 022, 609 667 246; www.catlanza.com), a luxury 23m (75ft) catamaran, is highly recommended. The Anglo-Irish-Canarian crew are great fun and will take you to Lanzarote's Papagayo beaches. *Siña María* is a German-run 18m (60ft) luxury catamaran, which specialises in sea fishing and operates from Corralejo. They anchor off Lobos for snorkelling and swimming (tel: 686 725 327).

By Land
The number one bike centre is **Easy Riders** in the Calle Las Dunas (tel: 928 867 005). The bike specialist hikes out bikes and offers guided day trips catering to different levels of competence.

WALKING

The Sendero de Bayuyo is very impressive, leading from Lajares through a strange volcanic landscape to the Calderón Hondo crater (▶142). Hannelore von der Twer offers guided tours (tel. 608 928 380, www.living-atlantis.de).

The Centre

Getting Your Bearings	66
Two Perfect Days	68
Top 10	70
At Your Leisure	75
Where to...	79

☀ Little Treats

Medicinal plants in the semi-desert
To the south of Antigua in Tiscamanita (➤ 79) is an **aloe vera farm**. You can visit the facilities and buy products in the factory.

Luxurious spa
The **Fuerteventura Thalasso Spa in** Caleta de Fuste (➤ 75) promises pure relaxation.

Cheese-tasting
Near the old capital of Betancuria (➤ 70), you can try out and buy **local goat's cheese** directly from the manufacturer.

The Centre

Getting Your Bearings

The interior of Fuerteventura is home to spectacular mountain scenery and the villages of Betancuria, Vega de Río Palmas, Pájara and Antigua are the oldest and among the most picturesque on the island. You can trace their history through their beautiful churches and colonial architecture and as a bonus they also have some of the finest places to eat.

While Betancuria is a monument to Fuerteventura's major historical events, the Ecomuseo de La Alcogida at Tefía is the no-less-fascinating story of how ordinary *majoreros* have eked a living from this harsh land over the last century or so. The drive from Tefía via Betancuria to Pájara is along one of the most beautiful stretches of countryside on the island, and there are frequent *miradores* (viewing points) from which to enjoy the ancient landscape.

On the east coast the proximity of the airport and the man-made resort of Caleta de Fuste means it's very popular with British holidaymakers. To the north lies the tourist-free capital of Puerto del Rosario while just south the delightful little fishing hamlet of Salinas del Carmen is worth a visit, not only for its peaceful location but also for its recently opened Salt Museum.

The west coast is wild unadulterated Fuerteventura, as exemplified by Playa de Garcey where the *SS American Star* was wrecked and the giant Caleta Negra cave north of Ajuy. Don't miss visiting these shores but never underestimate the power of the sea – the sea along the beaches is far too dangerous for swimmers.

Windmills await the visitors to the centre of the island

Getting Your Bearings

At Your Leisure

- 15 Los Molinos ➤ 75
- 16 Puerto del Rosario ➤ 75
- 17 Caleta de Fuste ➤ 75
- 18 Salinas del Carmen ➤ 76
- 19 Vega de Río Palmas ➤ 76
- 20 Ajuy ➤ 77
- 21 Pájara ➤ 77
- 22 Centro de Interpretación de los Molinos ➤ 78
- 23 Gran Tarajal & Las Playitas ➤ 78

TOP 10

- ⭐ Betancuria ➤ 70
- ⭐ Antigua ➤ 73
- ⭐ Ecomuseo de La Alcogida ➤ 74

67

The Centre

Two Perfect Days

This suggested itinerary offers a good way to visit some of the most interesting sights in the centre of Fuerteventura in just two days. For more information see the main entries (➤ 70–78).

Day One

Morning
From **17 Caleta de Fuste** head north, bypass **16 Puerto del Rosario**, drive inland towards Betancuria and Antigua on the FV20 then head north to spend the rest of the morning at the ⭐**Ecomuseo de La Alcogida** (➤ 74) at Tefia. Head west for a late fish lunch at **15 Los Molinos** (➤ 75).

Afternoon
Retrace your journey back to the FV20, head towards Betancuria, but after passing through Valle de Santa Inés, turn off the road towards ⭐**Antigua** (photo right) and visit the **22 Centro de Interpretacíon de los Molinos** (➤ 78).

Head back east on the FV50 and FV2, which emerges on the coast at **18 Salinas del Carmen** (➤ 76). Visit the Salt Museum and enjoy dinner or just a drink at **Los Caracolitos** restaurant (➤ 80).

Two Perfect Days

Day Two

Morning
Drive straight to ⭐**Betancuria** (photo left, ➤70) and spend the morning visiting the church, the Museo de Arte Sacro and the Casa Santa María. Have lunch in either one of the **Casa Santa María's cafés** or at the equally impressive **Don Antonio** (➤81) at ⓱ **Vega de Río Palmas** (➤76).

Afternoon
Head south through Vega de Río Palmas towards Pájara. Before visiting the famous church, turn right in the village centre and follow the signs to ⓴ **Ajuy** (➤77) where you can walk along the shore of the very first part of the Canarian archipelago that rose from the seas millions of years ago. If you haven't eaten yet there are also good fish restaurants here. Head back to ㉑ **Pájara** (➤77) by which time the church will be open. You can dine just across the road in **La Fonda restaurant** (➤81).

General note
See also the suggested drive, which links several of the places we feature in the central part of the island (➤145–149).

The Centre
⭐ 2 Betancuria

Once the island capital and still retaining a real sense of history, the village of Betancuria is Fuerteventura's principal place of interest. You can see all its "sights" in a couple of hours but take your time. Wander around the houses – several of which have facades and doorways dating from the 16th and 17th centuries – then linger over a coffee or a meal and savour the atmosphere. Betancuria has some of the best places to eat and drink on the island.

The best way to approach Betancuria is from the south. Just as you enter the village, there's the famous picture-postcard view across the dry riverbed of the 17th-century church of Santa María, surrounded by a cluster of equally venerable bright white buildings streaked green by palm trees. The island conqueror, Jean de Béthencourt (▶ 13), founded his capital here in 1404, well away from the coast, with the intention of avoiding Berber pirate attacks. Unfortunately, the raiders were undeterred and in 1593 they destroyed the church and took 600 islanders as slaves. The village remained the capital until 1834 but thereafter became a sleepy backwater until the advent of tourism gave it a fresh lease of life.

THE PIRATE CANNON
The bronze cannon in the front garden of the **Museo Arqueológico** was seized from the British at the Battle of Tamasite (near Tuineje). In 1740 a troop of English privateers attacked the island. The inhabitants managed to fight off the privateers and took the cannon as booty. (▶ 21)

A view of Betancuria

Betancuria

Iglesia de Santa María
Rebuilt in 1620, this is one of the most beautiful churches on the island, with naïve-style pastel-painted side altars providing relief from the baroque high altar. The church has Gothic arches, a wine-glass-shaped pulpit, a *mudéjar* ceiling, and a Judgement Day painting. Centuries-old gravestones form part of the uneven flagged floor, and the Norman image of St Catherine is one of the oldest post-conquest relics in the archipelago. The church is no longer used for services.

The restored Casa Santa María is an island showcase

Casa Santa María
Set opposite the church, at first glance you might think that the Casa Santa María is no more than an extremely attractive restaurant and café (➤ 79). In fact this is just a small part of the largest house in the village, much of it dating from the 16th century. It was restored by its German owner to become an island showcase in the 1990s. To access the rest of the house you have to walk alongside the restaurant to the **Museo Artesanía** entrance. Here, beautifully arranged in a series of Spanish colonial-style wooden and stone rooms, terraces and courtyards decked with flowers and greenery, you will find island merchandise for sale, tasting areas, a video and exhibition of rural bygones, artisans at work, a cactus garden and perhaps the prettiest café on the island. Don't miss the multivision audio-visual show, which features the brilliant photography of Reiner Loos and Luis Soltmann.

Museo de Arte Sacro
The collection of religious art is normally housed in the colonial building opposite the Iglesia de Santa María. Since this was closed when it fell into disrepair, the most important exhibits have been displayed at the parish church. Its highlights are the figure of Santiago (St James), brought by the Spanish in the hope that it might evangelise the Guanches, and the Pendón de la Conquista, Béthencourt's original flag.

INSIDER INFO

- Come here **early or late** to beat the coach tours, but not on a Sunday when most things are closed.
- The 20-minute **Casa Santa María** Multivision audio-visual show will whet your appetite for seeing the whole island. There is no commentary (just music) so no language difficulty! *Insider Tip*

Convento de San Buenaventura
Set 200m north of the church in a gully just off the main road is the roofless ruin of the Convento de San Buenaventura. This Franciscan abbey was the oldest on the island, founded by monks who came over with the Norman conquerors. Its roof collapsed in 1836, however, and the monks moved away.

Museo Arqueológico
The highlight of this rather uninspiring collection of Guanche relics is its display from La Cueva de los Idolos (the Cave of the Idols) in Villaverde. Pick up a booklet from the desk, which translates the Spanish captions into other languages.

TAKING A BREAK

See ➤ 79–81 for the several restaurant options in and around Betancuria.

Picturesque ruins: the former Franciscan cloister

🞢 164 C5

Iglesia de Santa María & Museo de Arte Sacro
✉ Calle Carmelo Silvera
☎ 928 878 003 🕒 Tue–Sat 10–6 💶 €2

Casa Santa María
✉ Casa Santa María Museo Artesanía (Multivision, crafts and shops)
☎ 928 878 282 🕒 Mon–Sat 11–4 💶 €6

Museo Arqueológico
✉ Calle Roberto Roldán (main road)
☎ 928 862 342 🕒 Mon–Sat 12:30–3:50 💶 €1.50

③ Antigua

Antigua has many things in common with its close neighbour, Betancuria, across the mountain range. It is indeed an old *(antigua)* village, established in 1485 by settlers from Normandy and Andalucía, and it too was capital of the island, but only held that honour for a short while – either one year or 25 years, depending on which definition of capital you wish to use! Today it is a well-kept village, although it doesn't attract as many visitors as Betancuria. It does, however, have the most visited windmill on the island.

The centre of Antigua features a charming square with the pretty white church of **Nuestra Señora de Antigua**, built in 1785. Hoopoes fly around the gardens in the square.

Just north of the village is the **Molino de Antigua**, a mini-village museum and exhibition centre, constructed under the supervision of Lanzarote's inspirational architect and artist César Manrique (➤ 108). The centrepiece is a beautifully restored 200-year-old windmill set in a botanical garden with Canarian flora and cacti from all over the world. The Centro also includes a craft centre and shop, the **Majorero Cheese Museum**, opened in 2014, and a pleasant little plaza with a café. La Molina restaurant (currently closed) was integrated into a large round granary. This can be visited.

Antigua boasts the most visited windmill on the island

TAKING A BREAK
The **cafeteria** in the **Molino de Antigua** is perfect for a break, whether for a small snack or a good coffee.

✚ 164 C5

Molino de Antigua
✉ In the village centre ☎ 928 862 342 ⏰ Tue–Sat 10–6 💶 €5

INSIDER INFO

Some areas of the **Centro** may be closed due to staff shortages. This is also a popular venue with coach parties so it may be crowded.

The Centre

⭐ 7 Ecomuseo de La Alcogida

This 🏛 open-air museum, set in the red-dust countryside, is a slice of rural village island life as it was some 50 to 100 years ago. There are five houses and farms to visit so allow a couple of hours to see everything.

The first house is a typical example of a simply furnished "modest family house". Set in a stone shed-like building, a film (in Spanish only) explains how the houses were reconstructed in the 1990s. Señor Teodisio's house is an example of "a well-to-do family house", with a camel and two donkeys tethered in front of it. The third farm comprises five buildings, one of which houses a donkey-powered mill or *tahona*. A museum attendant harnesses a donkey every few minutes to demonstrate how this works. Beware if you're inside the *tahona* barn at the time as dust and grain flies everywhere! Another house is devoted to craft workers (including cane workers, potters, weavers and stonemasons).

An ***alcogida*** is an irrigation ditch or canal, vital in collecting and distributing what little water can be gathered by precipitation or pumped from the ground.

Learn about traditional crafts and lifestyles at the Ecomuseo de La Alcogida

TAKING A BREAK

The reception area includes a dark low-ceilinged little café-bar where locals gather. You can get a drink here and perhaps a freshly baked aniseed-flavoured bread roll. The nearest recommended restaurant is at **Los Molinos** (▶ 80).

➕ 162 C2
✉ Tefía ☎ 928 878 049
🕐 Tue–Sat 10–6 💶 €5

INSIDER INFO

Pick up an **audio device** with a commentary in English. **Take care when crossing the main road**. Not a lot of traffic comes this way but it can be fast. Also beware low roofs and do not get in the way of the *tahona* (donkey-powered mill) when it starts working!

At Your Leisure

15 Los Molinos
A picturesque spot, popular with locals and tourists, the little fishing village of Los Molinos is one of the few places on the island where you will see fresh running water. A footbridge crosses a shallow slow-flowing stream making its way to a small lagoon, and a flock of ducks, joined by the occasional wading bird, sits in front of the Restaurant Casa Pon. Around the corner, right on the beach, is La Terraza, another good bet for a fish lunch (➤ 80). In summer the beach is golden sand; in winter the waves wash it away to uncover black shingle.
✛ 162 B2

16 Puerto del Rosario
Arguably the main attraction of the island capital are the modern sculptures set up all over the town and along the harbour road as part of a symposium on sculpture. You can get a street map at the tourist centre that shows you where to find the individual works. The town's main church is the pastel-blue **Iglesia Nuestra Señora del Rosario**, built in 1830. Adjacent is the **Casa Museo Unamumo**. This was formerly the modest Hotel Fuerteventura where the poet Miguel Unamuno (➤ 76) spent most of his time on the island, and there is a small exhibition of memorabilia and furnishing of the period.

On the corner of Calle Primero Mayo and Calle Jesús y Mary is the Cafeteria Naufragio. Pop in here to see salvaged materials from the ill-fated luxury liner *SS American Star* (➤ 32).
✛ 163 E1

Sculpture at the harbour of Puerto del Rosario

Casa Museo Unamuno
✉ Calle Virgen del Rosario
☎ 928 862 376 🕒 Mon–Fri 9–2 💰 Free

17 Caleta de Fuste
The methodically laid out tourist town, with its big hotels, bungalow complexes and shopping centres, is built around a shallow protected bay and a busy little port. It was previously known simply as El Castillo after the Castillo de Fuste, a squat black stone watchtower built in 1741, now appropriated by the Hotel Barceló as the

The Centre

centrepiece of an outdoor swimming pool complex. A few metres away, overlooking the port, is a black stone lighthouse.

The 🏖 **beach** is man-made but very family friendly and ideal for learning windsurfing. The port has a small aquarium (➤84).
⊞ 165 F4

🔟 Salinas del Carmen
Salinas are saltpans and have been worked at this site since the 18th century. The current pans date from 1910 and were in use until just a few years ago. They have been restored as part of the new **Museo de la Sal**. *Insider Tip*

Outside the museum interpretive boards tell how the salt was dried, cleaned and stored in the newly restored *almacen* (warehouse) then moved on wagons on rails into boats at the quiet little fishing hamlet just 100m away. Mounted above the saltpans is the eye-catching 15m-long (50ft) skeleton of a whale, which beached here recently. The pans and the bay attract several species of wading birds.
⊞ 165 F4

Museo de la Sal
☎ 928 174 926 ⓘ Tue–Fri, Sun 9:30–5:30

🔟 Vega de Río Palmas
This is one of the island's most fertile valleys, dotted with mini oases of palm trees watered by water pumps which delve deep beneath the baked top soil. Reservoirs are a rare sight on Fuerteventura but from a vantage

---

THE CONTROVERSIAL POET

Don Miguel Unamuno was born in Bilbao in 1864. In 1900 he was elected rector of Salamanca University, Spain's most distinguished seat of learning, from where he pursued his love of poetry and philosophy. Ever the outspoken republican, he was dismissed from his post because of his criticism of the king, and in March 1924 as a result of his vociferous opposition to the Spanish Premier, Primo de Rivera, he was exiled to Fuerteventura. He was here just four months before fleeing to Paris where he stayed until 1930, returning to Spain when Rivera fell from power. At the outbreak of the civil war, Unamuno sided with Franco but soon fell out with him and was placed under house arrest where he died in 1936. Despite his brief sojourn on Fuerteventura, Unamuno developed a real affinity with its spartan beauty and simple lifestyle, "a rock thirsting in the sun... .a treasure of health and honesty" and often referred to the island in his writing. As he is the only man of letters ever to be associated with Fuerteventura, the authorities have not surprisingly made a fuss of him, and his most famous quote "Fuerteventura is an oasis in the desert of civilization" has become a mantra in island guidebooks and tourist literature. A statue of Unamuno can be seen at the foot of Montaña Quemada (➤146).

At Your Leisure

point high on the main road you can spot the **Embalse de la Peñitas** and the little white chapel of La Virgen de la Peña (➤ 147).

The village church, the **Ermita de La Virgen de la Peña**, dates from the late 18th century and is worth a look inside. On the third Saturday in September this is the focal point for one of the island's most colourful fiestas (➤ 19).

🟥 164 B4

Ermita de la Virgen de la Peña
✉ Located in the centre of the village
🕐 Tue–Sun 11–1, 5–7

20 Ajuy

In 1402 the Norman invaders, led by Jean de Béthencourt, first landed on Fuerteventura. Today it is a quiet fishing village also known by the name of Puerto Peña, mostly visited for its black sand beach, popular with surfers, and its fish restaurants. The local fishing fleet only operate between May and October, as in winter the sea is too rough.

Take a walk up the steps and along the cliff edge to see how the wind and waves have carved strange patterns. Further north you will find what is referred to as the natural monument of 🟥 **Caleta Negra** with an impressive cave just

> **ISLAND CHURCH INTERIORS**
> The island's charming 18th-century churches (including those at Betancuria, Antigua, La Oliva and Pájara) share a number of very similar characteristics: a wine glass-shaped pulpit, a painting of Christ in Majesty (with souls below in Hell), and an intricate wooden Moorish-style ceiling.

above the water. Even experienced cave-goers should be careful when descending from here, and even more so if the sea is rough.

🟥 164 A4

21 Pájara

You'll find Pájara looking spick and span and a welcome burst of floral colour after the stark brown hues of the interior. It is one of the island's oldest villages, settled in the 17th century and famous for its church, **Nuestra Señora de la Regla**, built in 1685. The carvings on the portal depict what appear to be two native Indians in headdresses, plus stylised birds and animals. These are often referred to as Aztec-influenced and while the material and the style of carving indicate a local craftsperson, the origins of the style is a mystery. Pájara is also the village nearest

Vega de Río Palmas is one of the island's greenest spots

With its graduated houses, Las Playitas is one of the prettiest places in this area

to the famous but no longer visible shipwreck *SS American Star* (➤ 33).
✚ 164 B4

22 Centro de Interpretación de los Molinos

This area was once the "breadbasket" of the interior so it's an appropriate place for a Windmill Interpretation Centre. The exhibition is based in a lovely old restored house and garden and includes hand mills, animal-powered mills and windmills, including a full-sized one you can enter. Pick up a leaflet to translate the captions into your own language.

✚ 165 C4
✉ Calle la Cruz 13, Tiscamanita (Tuineje)
☎ 928 164 275 🕓 Tue–Sat 10–6 💶 €2

INSIDER INFO

Five good fish restaurants
Casa Victor, Las Playitas (➤ 81)
Frasquita, Caleta de Fuste (➤ 80)
Puerto de la Peña (Casa Pepin), Ajuy (➤ 81)
La Terraza, Los Molinos (➤ 80)
Los Caracolitos, Salinas del Carmen (➤ 81)

23 Gran Tarajal/Las Playitas

Although it is the second biggest town on the island after Puerto del Rosario, there is little to attract visitors to Gran Tarajal aside from a large, well-kept, black sand beach. It's better to make a beeline 6km (3.5mi) north to the little white fishing village of Las Playitas, with less manicured dark sands but more character and popular fish restaurants. From Las Playitas, a narrow cul-de-sac leads to the **Faro de Entallada**. The lookout point besides the lighthouse provides a wonderful view of the island's east coast.
✚ 164 C1/165 D2

78

Where to...
Eat and Drink

Prices
Expect to pay for a three-course meal for one, excluding drinks and service
€ under €15   €€ €15–€25   €€€ over €25

BETANCURIA

Casa Princess Arminda €€
Set in an atmospheric 16th-century building in the historic heart of the village, the Casa Princess Arminda features typical Canarian dishes which are mostly home made, featuring local and sometimes home-grown ingredients. Try the speciality lamb stew, packed with fresh herby flavours, and finish with the house dessert special, banana and almond cake.
🖶 165 C5 ✉ Calle Juan de Bethencourt, 2
☎ 928 87 89 79; www.princessarminda.com

Casa Santa María Café Bar (inside Museo Artesanía) €€
Take a seat on the terrace beneath a thatched parasol or under the laurel tree surrounded by bougainvillea, a lemon tree and an immaculate **cactus garden**. It's rather like sitting in a picture postcard complete with smiling waitress in traditional dress. Snacks include smoked pork fillet, Lanzarote smoked salmon and mackerel fillets.
🖶 165 C5
✉ Plaza Iglesia ☎ 928 878 282
🕐 Mon–Sat 11–4. Note: you have to pay to get into the Museo Artesanía (➤ 71) but it is well worth the admission.

Casa Santa María Restaurant €€€ *Insider Tip*
The Casa Santa María Restaurant is in the dining room of a gloriously restored 16th-century farmhouse. Antiques abound though don't overpower and the food is first class, although it can be expensive (there is a daily set menu at a more reasonable price). Start with dates in bacon or fresh cheese baked with tomatoes and garlic. House specials are lamb and kid and a range of local dishes. Finish with a hot apple strudel or chocolate tart with mango sorbet.
🖶 165 C5
✉ Plaza Iglesia ☎ 928 878 282
🕐 Daily 11–4

Val Tarajal €€
This traditional dark-wood restaurant has few frills except for a giant 4m (13ft) long *timple* (Canarian five-string ukulele-like instrument) on one wall! All the usual Canarian favourites are on the menu but if you want *puchero* or *sancocho* (➤ 25) you'll have to come on Sunday or public holidays.
🖶 165 C5
✉ Calle Roberto Roldán 6 (main road)
☎ 928 878 007 🕐 Sun–Fri 10–4:30

ANTIGUA

La Molina €€
It feels almost as if you are stepping inside a huge windmill as you enter this large round building. In fact, it used to be a granary. It has been beautifully restored with brown and white giraffe-patterned bare stone walls and gleaming woodwork. Rustic candelabras have been made from inverted clay pots riddled with holes through which the light shines, and with Canarian music playing in the background this completes the

The Centre

ambience. The food is upmarket traditional island cuisine. Start with fried cheese with *mojo verde* or *carpaccio* of tuna. Then try goat stew or *cazuela de pescadores*, a special fish stew.
✚ 164 C5
✉ Carretera de Antigua km20 ☎ 928 878 041
🕐 Currently shut due to renovation work

PUERTO DEL ROSARIO

El Cangrejo Colorao €€
This restaurant is located in a concealed blind alley north of the harbour. It is not very far to walk if you have just visited the art centre (Centro de Arte Juan Ismael) in the Calle Almirante Lallermand. The restaurant name means red crab, an indicator that it is mainly fish and seafood that is served here. The style of the restaurant may seem a little old-fashioned but the terrace is directly on the waterfront and provides a clear view of the activities in the harbour.
✚ 163 E1
✉ Calle Juan Ramón Jimenez 2
☎ 928 858 477

LOS MOLINOS

La Terraza €€
This is the best of the two fish restaurants in this pretty little fishing village and, unlike its neighbour, it enjoys a grandstand view over the beach. There's not much sophistication here, with plastic tables and chairs, but the service is good.
✚ 162 B2
✉ Los Molinos 🕐 Wed–Mon noon–7

CALETA DE FUSTE

Frasquita €€
"Only Fresh Fish" is the motto at this rustic no-frills whitewashed landmark beachside restaurant on the opposite side of the bay from the port. Choose your fish from a tray brought to you by the waiter – it's unlikely to be expensive and the best quality is guaranteed.
✚ 165 F4 ✉ Playa Caleta de Fuste
☎ 928 586 998 🕐 Tue–Sun 1–4, 6–9

Gambrinus €€
Nominally a *cervecería* ("beer house") with an old beer lorry outside and with a beery feel to its dark wood-panelled interior, Gambrinus is actually a large smart modern restaurant with rather formal pink tablecloths and wicker furniture that spill out onto a terrace. Steaks on hot stones and flambés are the specialities but you'll be equally welcome for tapas, pizza, a cocktail or just a beer. Live music daily in summer.
✚ 165 F4 ✉ CC Broncemar
☎ 928 163 555 🕐 Daily 9am–11pm

Puerto Castillo El Faro €€
The restaurant is on the first floor of the harbour building, and the large terrace offers a fine view of the yacht harbour and the sickle-shaped beach. Mediterranean dishes such as paella and various fish specialities feature on the menu as does *Escalope alla Romana*. There is also a very respectable choice of wines.
✚ 165 F4 ✉ Puerto deportivo
☎ 928 949 835 🕐 Daily 5pm–11:30pm

La Paella €€–€€€
Recently opened, La Paella which belongs to Hotel Barceló Puerto Castillo, hopes to make a name for itself among the leading restaurants in the area, which is reflected in the high prices. Naturally paella features high on the menu but other Mediterranean specialities are not neglected. The location directly by the beach could not be better.
✚ 165 F4 ✉ Paseo de la Playa
☎ 928 163 100 🕐 Daily 1:30–10:30

SALINAS DEL CARMEN

Los Caracolitos €€
This attractive little modern restaurant sits almost right on the

Where to...

beach of this tiny fishing hamlet. There is a reasonable choice of fish and seafood dishes on the menu but if you want to go local start with the home-made fish croquettes then ask for the catch of the day. The staff are friendly and helpful.
🕂 165 F4 ✉ Salinas del Carmen
☎ 928 174 242 🕒 Mon–Sat noon–11
🚫 No credit cards

VEGA DE RÍO PALMAS

Don Antonio €€€ *Insider Tip*
Housed in a lilac-trimmed colonial house opposite the church, is not only pretty from without, but also from within – its courtyard and dining rooms are stunning. It may be the most expensive restaurant on the island but the food and surroundings are unbeatable. A short menu of nouvelle international-Canarian-Spanish dishes changes daily. Gourmets with deep wallets will appreciate the *menú degustación* (selection of dishes) of five or seven courses.
🕂 164 B4 ✉ Plaza Iglesia
☎ 928 878 757 🕒 Tue–Sun 10–5

AJUY

Puerto de la Peña (Casa Pepin) €€
Either of the two restaurants on the front at Ajuy are fine for fresh fish and seafood, but, if you would like to eat with the locals, try the Puerto de la Peña. It has the added ingredient of Pepin, a colourful local character who will (normally) be delighted to show you the interior of his house.
🕂 164 A4 ✉ Puerto Aziel
☎ 928 161 529, 628 671 004 🕒 Daily 10–5

Jaula de Oro €
Of all the restaurants in the town, this simple beach restaurant which calls itself "Golden Cage" is the closest to the waterfront. In a relaxed atmosphere, guests are served no-frills but delicious fish dishes, and the prices are extremely reasonable. If you are not very hungry, you can order tapas.
🕂 164 A4 ☎ 928 161 594
🕒 Tue–Sun 10–6

PÁJARA

Bar Restaurant La Fonda €€
Just across the road from the church, La Fonda is patronised by locals who drink in its rustic bar and tourists who eat outside beneath the trees. There's a selection of tapas and Canarian favourites to choose from including house specials *carne mechada* (slices of sirloin), *conejo en adobo* (marinated rabbit) and *garbanzos compuestos* (chickpea stew).
🕂 164 B4 ✉ Calle Nuestra Señora de Regla
☎ 928 161 625 🕒 Mon–Fri 9–6, Sat–Sun 9–9

Centro Cultural €
As long as you don't expect any culinary flights of fancy in this restaurant by the parish church, you will enjoy the reasonably priced local cuisine, which includes the usual favourites such as kid and rabbit, which are best accompanied by an island wine from Tenerife or Lanzarote.
🕂 164 B4 ✉ Plaza del Ayuntamiento
☎ 928 161 440 🕒 Daily 8am–midnight

LAS PLAYITAS

Casa Victor €€ *Insider Tip*
This is by no means the most attractive restaurant in Las Playitas but even when the rest of the village is deserted Victor's is buzzing. It has indoor dining only so it has to try that bit harder in terms of quality of food – fish and seafood being the staple items. A widespread reputation and a mixed clientele of locals, businessmen and tourists seem to indicate they have got it right.
🕂 165 D2 ✉ Calle Juan Soler 22
☎ 928 870 910 🕒 Tue–Sun noon–5, 8–11v

The Centre

Where to...
Stay

Prices
Expect to pay per double room, per night
€ under €60   €€ €60–€90   €€€ €91–€120   €€€€ over €120

Note that many of the larger hotels and apartments in Caleta de Fuste are block booked by big tour operators.

ANTIGUA

Hotel Era de la Corte €€–€€€
This beautiful *hotel rural* dates from 1890 and has been lovingly restored. All 11 rooms are individually furnished and have their own style and personality; several have four-poster beds. The ever-helpful owner is extremely knowledgeable on island life and has a small library specialising in Canary Island history, flora and fauna, where guests can relax with a book and a glass of wine. There are two small swimming pools, a solarium, garden and tennis court. Bicycles are available for rent; games provided include petanque, darts and table tennis. Breakfast is included in the price of the room.
165 C4 ✉ Calle La Corte 1
☎ 928 878 705, 928 878 708; www.eradelacorte.com

CALETA DE FUSTE

Hotel Elba Palace Golf €€€€
The 5-star hotel, located within the Golf Club Fuerteventura (➤42, 84), features every mod con but is designed in classic Canarian style. Its large inner courtyard is decked with palms and wooden balconies and even the staff uniform is based on traditional 18th-century Canarian dress. Its 51 bedrooms are luxurious, designed with local touches, and guest facilities include two large swimming pools, a floodlit tennis (or paddle tennis) court, Jacuzzi, sauna, steam bath and beauty treatments plus a gourmet restaurant.
165 F4 ✉ Urb, Fuerteventura Golf Club
☎ 928 163 922; www.hoteleselba.com

Barceló Puerto El Castillo €€€€
Get the best of both worlds by staying in pretty little white apartments in lush manicured gardens right on the sea front, with the back-up of a huge resort-hotel. This comes complete with an entertainment programme, bars, restaurants, pizzeria, creperie, ice cream shop, the Fuerteventura Thalasso Spa (with a jacuzzi and thalassotherapy), and a choice of five pools including the pretty one by the 18th-century Castillo (➤76) as well as a wide range of sports facilities.
165 F4 ✉ Avenida del Castillo
☎ 928 163 042; www.barcelo.com

Fuerteventura Thalasso Spa
☎ 928 160 961 ❶ Daily 10–6

PÁJARA

Hotel Rural Casa Isaítas €€
This charming, friendly, small hotel, set just outside the village, has four rooms simply furnished in "minimalist-rustic" style. Facilities include a library, internet access and a living room. Its restaurant is open to non-residents and is recommended. Breakfast is included.
164 B4 ✉ Calle Guize 7
☎ 928 161 402; www.casaisaitas.com

Where to…
Shop

BETANCURIA

Despite its name, the **Museo Artesanía in the Casa Santa María** is one of the best one-stop souvenir and gift shops on the island. It features tasting areas and beautiful displays of food and drink.

For ceramics, look in the **Ceramica Casa Santa María**, a busy little shop that is part of the same enterprise but has a different entrance (on the side street leading to the Museo Sacro).

Another good place for handicrafts is the **Centro Insular de Artesanía** on the main road.

On the southern edge of the village is the **Casa de Queso** (House of Cheese), a mini-supermarket selling a range of cured meats and cheeses.

Just outside the villages in the local cheese maker **Finca Pepe** (Granja la Acaravaneras, daily 10–6; www.fincapepe.com), where you can try the local goat's cheese and buy what takes your fancy.

ANTIGUA

There are a number of Centros Insular de Artesanía (government-funded Island Handicraft Centres) around the island, the largest one being at the Centro Molino at Antigua. These feature a range of typical island crafts. Items are often expensive but remember they are handmade, often requiring several hours' labour.

The largest is the **Centro Molino** in Antigua. The craft shop is one of the best on the island. You can buy beautiful (but very expensive) leather bags, craft jewellery, super-sized wooden geckoes, silkscreen and parchment pictures and some lovely pottery pieces.

PUERTO DEL ROSARIO

Puerto del Rosario caters solely for islanders. If you want to see what the locals are buying take a stroll along Calle Primero de Mayo and Calle León y Castillo, though most of the shops are old-fashioned and uninspiring.

One exception is **Las Rotondas** (Calle Francisco Pi y Arsuaga 2), which has a sales area of 30,000m² (323,000ft²) and with more than 100 businesses is the largest consumer temple on the island.

On the second Sunday of each month (10:30–2:30) a **craft market** is held in the village of Tetir 8km (5mi) west of Puerto del Rosario, selling leather goods, textiles, pottery, food and other local items.

CALETA DE FUSTE

Despite, or perhaps because of its many shopping centres, the standard of shopping in Caleta de Fuste is mediocre and usually price driven. The best shopping centre is the **Atlántico** directly on the main road.

Riu Parfum in the CC Castillo Plaza is the best bet for perfumes. The **island market** (➤ 42) comes to Caleta on Saturday morning.

BEAUTIFUL GOAT'S CHEESE

Fuerteventura is famous for its goat's cheese and has even succeeded in registering a Denominación de Origen classification (similar to the French Appellation Contrôlée wine system) to protect it from imitations. You can usually buy it in one of three ways: *natural*, its rind rubbed with oil to preserve it; *pimenta*, its rind rubbed with red pimenta (chilli pepper); or *gofio*, coated in toasted cornmeal.

The Centre

Where to...
Go Out

NIGHTLIFE

Good places to go in the evening are **Caleta de Fuste**, the **Blues Bar** in Centro Castillo and **Luna Blue**, a cocktail lounge with live music in the Hotel Elba Castillo Suite.

Of course for the real action, you need to go to the island capital of **Puerto del Rosario**

Young city dwellers go to the **Mama Rumba** (Calle San Roque 7), probably the most popular latino disco on the island, or **Camelot** (Calle León y Castillo 12).

There are 90 different beers to choose from at the **Heineken Bar** (Calle León y Castillo 146).

La Tierra (Calle Eustaqio Gopar) has live jazz on Friday and Saturday.

GOLF

For golf players, **Caleta de Fuste**, an 18-hole course, is the top address on the island.

Professional players also use the **Fuerteventura Golf Club** (tel: 928 160 034; www.fuerteventura golfclub.com) in the south of the holiday resort, which was opened in 2002.

Not far away is the **Salinas de Antigua** (tel: 928 877 272, www. salinasgolf.com), another 18-hole golf course, which also has a golf hotel and golf school.

And then there is also the **Las Playitas Golf** course near Gran Tarajal. This 18-hole club with four small lakes, a PGA golf academy and a sport hotel was designed by the golf course architect John Chilver Stainer.

SEA EXCURSIONS

The most interesting of these is the **Oceanarium Explorer** *(Insider Tip)* based in Caleta de Fuste. Before setting off in the glass-bottomed boat you visit an **aquarium** where there are sharks and rays and an octopus that has been taught to unscrew a glass jar. Children can feed and stroke some of the animals, as well as swim with a trained sea lion if they wish. If you don't like the idea of going out on the boat, you can actually see quite a few fish from the walkway.

WATER SPORTS

The sheltered bay of Caleta de Fuste is an ideal place to take your first windsurfing lessons. The Fanatic Fun Centre will get you going.

For diving contact the German-led **Deep Blue** (tel: 928 163 712; www.deep-blue-diving.com), who have 20 years experience here.

GO-KARTING

The **Tamaretilla Karting Club** (tel: 620 504 399) offers a 1,500m adult circuit and shorter courses for juniors and children. It is near the village of Cardón, close to Tuineje.

HORSERIDING

The **Finca Crines del Viento** (tel: 609 001 141; www.crines delviento.es) stables at Triquivijate, near Antigua, offers rides suitable for beginners and experienced riders. The staff speak English and German.

TRIKE TOURS

Cool Runnings (inside Centro Comercial El Castillo, tel: 649 938 581) offers guided trike tours leaving from Caleta de Fuste.

The South

Getting Your Bearings	86
Three Perfect Days	88
Top 10	90
At Your Leisure	96
Where to…	100

☼ Little Treats

Simple Pleasures
For example about 20km (12.5 mi) west of Morro Jable (➤97) in Puerto de la Cruz in **El Caletón**, a no-frills fish restaurant with a glorious view of the Atlantic.

On the rooftop of Fuerteventura
If you like walking, you can ascend the **Pico de la Zarza** from Jandía Playa (➤98).

Skeleton in the lighthouse
The **Faro de Jandía** lighthouse west of Morro Jable (➤97) has the 6m (20ft)-long skeleton of a fin whale dangling from the roof.

The South

Getting Your Bearings

La Pared (literally, "the wall"), the start of the isthmus, is both the historical boundary – where the ancient wall that divided the island's two kingdoms once stood (▶ 13) – and an important "geo-tourism" frontier. North of here the sands are volcanic black, a daunting prospect to most holidaymakers, but almost immediately south, beginning at Costa Calma, the longest, most famous and most beautiful golden-blonde beaches in the Canaries stretch for over 30km (18mi).

The new face of the south is Costa Calma, a man-made resort bristling with large modern hotels and shopping centres. On the beaches on the Jandía isthmus to the south west, tourism is focused around Jandía Playa. This seaside town has mushroomed into a large holiday resort over the last 40 years and merged with its neighbour, the former fishing town of Morro Jable. The advantage of this holiday region is that unlike the north of Fuerteventura, which can become quite cloudy, the sun shines on the isthmus for almost 365 days a year, which makes it ideal for beach and surfing holidays.

The north coast (Barlovento) of the isthmus provides a contrast to the holiday centres on the Playas de Jandía. You will hardly see a soul in this region, no hotel buildings have yet disfigured the kilometre-long beaches of Cofete.

Today the road to Morro Jable is the focus of construction works. Fast straight roads and 30m-high (100ft) bridges will make short work of the deep gullies which slow traffic to a zigzag crawl. The distance from north to south, in driving time at least, is shortening. For most holidaymakers, Morro Jable, an attractive spot with local life and a gorgeous beach, is the end of the line, and despite the new road-building programme will remain so for many years.

Camels in the La Lajita Oasis Park

Getting Your Bearings

TOP 10
★ Playas de Jandía ➤ 90
★ La Lajita Oasis Park ➤ 93

At Your Leisure
24 La Pared ➤ 96
25 Costa Calma ➤ 96
26 Jandía Playa ➤ 96
27 Morro Jable ➤ 97
28 Cofete ➤ 98

Popular places to visit include Morro Jable's beaches

Perfect Days in...

The South

Three Perfect Days

This suggested itinerary offers a good way to visit some of the most interesting sights in the south of Fuerteventura in just three days. For more information see the main entries (➤ 90–99).

Day One

Morning
Set out early, steal a march on the tour buses and arrive at ⭐ **8 La Lajita Oasis Park** (➤ 93) just as it opens at 9am. See all the shows and take lunch at the park in the Botanical Gardens area.

Afternoon
Drive north on the FV56 for 3–4km (2–3mi) and turn left towards La Pared passing through the hamlet of Las Hermosas. As the road approaches the coast there are tremendous views of the wild Barlovento coastline. At **24 La Pared** (➤ 96) you can sunbathe at the nearby Playa de la Pared (though swimming here is dangerous) and then enjoy an evening meal at **El Camello** (➤ 100).

Three Perfect Days

Day Two

Morning
Make your way to the El Palmeral centre on the main road at **25 Costa Calma** (➤ 96) and either walk or drive (you'll need an off-road vehicle) across the isthmus to the north coast following the route on pages 150–152. Return, have lunch at the **Fuerte Action bar** (➤ 100) and browse in the shops here.

Afternoon
Head south for 3–4km (2–3mi) and turn left to Risco del Paso where you can spend the rest of the day on the most famous stretch of beaches, the ⭐**Playas de Jandía** (➤ 90). You can windsurf or simply soak up the rays but remember to take your own shade along with you.

Day Three

Morning
You'll need an off-road vehicle and a sense of adventure for this excursion! Drive south past Morro Jable and take the signs to Cofete. After around 20km (12mi) you will arrive at a pass where stupendous views of the Barlovento coast make all the effort worthwhile. Continue for another 4km (2.5mi) into this remarkable landscape and you reach journey's end, the ramshackle hamlet of **28 Cofete** (photo left, ➤ 98) where you can get a rustic but enjoyable fish lunch.

Afternoon
Make your way back to "civilisation" at **27 Morro Jable** (➤ 97). Follow the signs to the Centro Urbano, park near the square in the old part of the village and spend the rest of the afternoon on the golden beach. Have dinner in one of the many restaurants or cafés on the square (➤ 102).

The South

★ Playas de Jandía

The beaches of Jandía are arguably Fuerteventura's greatest natural asset and certainly its most potent marketing tool. Water sports lovers, beach bums, families and naturists are all drawn here. Even if you have never been to Fuerteventura you've probably seen that picture, that golden yellow, seemingly endless beach. More rolls of film have been spent on the Sotavento than on any other beach in the Canary Islands and for sun worshippers it is definitely one of Europe's most attractive beaches.

There is still no hotel in the mountainous area of the Jandía Natural Park away from the coast, and hikers are increasingly discovering the raw beauty of this region.

The Sotavento Coast

The Playas de Jandía begins, with a whisper, in Costa Calma. Beyond the rows of blue-and-orange beach umbrellas and loungers the beach starts to broaden out, and at Playa Barca, by the landmark Meliá Gorriones hotel, it becomes extraordinary. Giant dunes rear out of black volcanic outcrops. A sandbar stretches for 5km (3mi) to Risco del Paso, taming the waves, making it perfect for families and novice windsurfers. The shallow

The Playas de Jandía are picture-postcard perfect

Playas de Jandía

> **BARLOVENTO AND SOTAVENTO**
> All the beaches on the 30km-long (18mi) south-east-facing coast from Costa Calma to Morro Jable are Sotavento, meaning leeward, though in fact the term Playa de Sotavento is only applied to a single small stretch. Similarly, the corresponding north-west-facing beaches of the peninsula are Barlovento or windward side, even though the term is only given to one stretch. Never swim on the Barlovento coastline, as even if the waters look calm there are treacherous undercurrents.

waters are a dozen ever-changing shades of blue and turquoise, gently lapping the golden-blonde streaks of sand. At Risco del Paso there is a beach bar, a water sports centre and a scattering of pretty white bungalows set well back from the beach on the low cliffs that form a backdrop. Walk along the beach for a couple of hundred metres and you will come to another favourite picture-postcard subject as a huge white dune and black volcanic cliffs tumble down to the sea. It is much easier to see where the Sotavento beach ends when you are high above, on the main road, as it is effectively marked by an unofficial *mirador*. From here you can enjoy the classic view.

Jandía Playa and Morro Jable

The next 3–4km (2–3mi) of sands is known as the Playa de Butihondo, still backed by low cliffs and shared by a number of large hotels and the German-owned holiday club resorts of Robinson and Aldiana. Set in manicured grounds they keep a discrete distance and so preserve the integrity of the beach.

As the coastline turns "the corner" from facing south east to due south it takes on its third name, Playa del Matorral, a sandy beach several hundred metres in width, bordered on the inside by salt marshes *(El Saladar)* now under protection.

The cliffs have disappeared by the time you get to Jandía Playa. Its landmark lighthouse (▶ 96) is impressive and, once past the resort, there is a final glorious flourish as once again the cliffs and dunes return and a beautiful promenade offers great views of the broad golden beach. This tapers down to end by the little square in Morro Jable and, for most people, this is the end of the Jandía beaches.

Beyond Jandía Playa

From here onwards you need a 4WD vehicle to explore the rest of the peninsula. By far the most popular drive, albeit a real bone-cruncher of a journey, is north to Cofete (▶ 98) where there is a fabulous

The South

long, untouched, empty golden beach. North east of here is the equally impressive Playa de Barlovento. Few people make it this far and nudity is the norm.

The easy way to visit the beaches of the northern coastline is to cross the peninsula at its narrowest point at Costa Calma, either by walking or by 4WD vehicle, following the simple route mapped out ➤ 150–152.

The wind on Playa de Sotavento lures many kitesurfers here

TAKING A BREAK

Insider Tip — There are good **beach bars** on two of the most attractive parts of the 30km-long (18mi) Sotavento beach, at Morro Jable (a five- to ten-minute walk from the centre) and at Risco del Paso.

✚ 167 E2–D1

INSIDER INFO

- Only at Costa Calma and part of Morro Jable will you find **beach shades** for rental. Anywhere else you will soon fry without some protection so invest in a parasol and, if you have small children, consider a small beach tent.

Getting there There are no signs to "Sotavento Beach". However, the start of it, the Playa Barca (Meliá Gorriones Hotel), is marked, as is the end, Risco del Paso. It's best to park at **Risco del Paso**. Keep your eyes peeled and your speed down as neither turn-off is particularly prominent.

⭐8 La Lajita Oasis Park

Oasis Park is the island's biggest, best and longest-running tourist attraction. It was established in 1985 as a small garden centre and even today first impressions are less a zoo than an oasis of vivid greenery and vibrant-coloured plants set in the middle of a barren red desert.

The park is distinguished by its fascinating animal life and verdant setting

The 🛝 Animal Park

The most interesting thing about this area is not so much its inhabitants, but the setting of their enclosures along narrow shady tracks with dense foliage, brightly coloured plants and running water. Children in particular will feel like jungle explorers. Among the hundreds of reptiles, primates and mammals and over 200 species of birds are crocodiles, tamarind monkeys, chimpanzees, meerkats, capybaras, toucans, turacos, ostriches, flamingos and pelicans.

Animal and bird shows

The parrot and *sea lion* shows are great fun for children even if some adults may take exception to what they see as unnatural behaviour. However, you won't doubt the courage of the crocodile tamer as he puts his head within

The South

inches of bone-crushing jaws. The birds of prey show draws on the park's large collection of raptors, which for one reason or another can sadly no longer survive in the wild, and has rather more educational over entertainment content. The sea lion show is great fun and there are also reptile-handling demonstrations.

Camel breeding

Camels were introduced to the islands in 1405 by the Normans (▶ 28) but by 1985 they had dwindled almost to extinction, numbering less than three dozen in total. Oasis Park is hoping to reintroduce herds of the true *camello majorero* (Fuerteventuran camel) by breeding the very few that are left with African dromedaries. The park also plans to set up the first camel milk dairy in Europe. High in protein, mineral and vitamin C content, but low in cholesterol, camel milk is said to be good for the liver and the complexion. The herd here is now 220-strong and a visit to see the beautiful baby camels is highly recommended.

THE CAMEL'S BEST SEATS
The yoke-like camel seat that accommodates two people is called *la silla inglesa*, the English chair, as it was specially designed for saddle-sore English tourists in the 19th century. An original handmade wooden *silla inglesa* is now a prized antique fetching well over €2,000 at auction.

You will see ostriches and camels...

La Lajita Oasis Park

...and how the crocodiles are fed

Camel rides *Insider Tip*
For most visitors this is a highlight of a visit to the park and involves two people being slung, one either side of the camel, in a yoke-like wooden seat reminiscent of a funfair ride. The ride is smooth and pleasant and ascends a steep hill with excellent views of the park gardens and out to sea. There is an extra charge for rides.

Botanic Garden
Set on a steep hillside in artfully arranged gardens of black volcanic pumice particles, this collection of over 1,500 different types of cactus, succulents and indigenous plants is one of the largest and most interesting in Europe. Don't be deterred if the prospect of a cactus garden seems literally and figuratively a dry idea. From dainty little ground-hugging plants with bright yellow and shocking pink flowers and soft downy spines to classic Mexican giants with needles that could skewer someone's hand, there's every kind of cactus under the sun here.

Out of Africa
A massive new African Savannah area has giraffes, antelopes and endangered African animals including rhinoceroses, though no big cats or other predators.

TAKING A BREAK
The park has three excellent restaurants.

167 F3
Carretera General de Jandía (FV2 km 57.4), La Lajita
902 400 434; www.lajitaoasispark.com
Daily 9–7:30 €25, children €12.50. Separate charge for camel rides

INSIDER INFO

- Arrive first thing in the cool of the early morning before the coach operators arrive and **wear comfortable shoes** – it's a long walk to see everything. Don't miss the **giraffes**, the **Botanic Garden**, the **baby camels** and the **crocodile show**. The **camel breeding area** is off the main track and may be closed to the general public. Call in advance and you may be allowed special access. Keep your eyes peeled in the free-flying bird aviary for a **large chameleon**.
- If you are travelling independently, park by the main zoo entrance. Inside the 250,000m² (62 acre) complex, there is a complimentary **shuttle bus service**, which will also take you to the **Botanic Garden**.

95

The South

At Your Leisure

24 La Pared

The site of the wall that once divided the island into two ancient kingdoms (➤ 13), La Pared today is home to an upmarket, largely German-populated *urbanización* (residential development). From the road above the village you can pick out the bizarre sight of bright green target circles on a black lava background. These are the greens of a nine-hole practice golf course. La Pared is also home to **El Camello**, one of the island's most attractive restaurants (➤ 100). Drive a little further north on the FV605 past the village turn-off and a superb panorama of the north coast opens out before you.

167 E3

25 Costa Calma

Built from scratch as an upmarket resort in the late 1970s and 1980s, Costa Calma is a disparate collection of shopping centres and large resort hotels that share the same golden sandy beach. This is the start of the famous **Playa de Sotavento** (➤ 90), though it is by no means the nicest stretch, where building continues apace.

167 E3

26 Jandía Playa

The ugly duckling of the south, this man-made mostly German-speaking resort is a cluster of large hotels and shopping centres facing onto the least interesting stretch of the Playa Matorral. The towering

---

Insider Tip

UNUSUAL ARCHITECTURE

Although much of the new architecture of the south (particularly its hotels) is instantly forgettable or completely out of place, there are three striking examples of truly individual properties that merit more than a second glance.

First, just north of **Esquinzo** stands a fantasy "gingerbread" house straight from the Brothers Grimm tales that sits almost next door to the Club Paraíso Playa Sunrise Beach Hotel.

Second, looking down on Costa Calma at its northern extremity is what appears to be a large church on top of a hill. In fact, it is part of the beautifully crafted Old-Spain pueblo (village)-style hotel of Rio Calma.

Third, at the southern end of Costa Calma is the extraordinary "space pod" complex of the Risco del Gato hotel (photo below, ➤ 103), which was actually one of the pioneer accommodations in the south.

96

Morro Jable is home to the island's largest lighthouse

Faro (lighthouse) **de Morro Jable** was built at the turn of the 20th century and is the largest on the island. The only other point of interest here is the small zoo in the gardens of the Hotel Stella Canaris (open daily 10–6; €8). A beautifully landscaped new promenade stretches from Jandía Playa to Morro Jable (➤ below).
🕂 167 D1

27 Morro Jable

This popular resort is the end of the line of Sotavento beaches (➤ 90) and features one of its best stretches. The broad golden sands, known as the **Playa de Cebada** (Barley Beach), are backed by a large dune and low cliffs, have lots of space and excellent facilities for sun worshippers including parasols and loungers for hire, a good beach bar and gleaming new stainless steel-and-glass toilet and shower facilities. There's a great view of it all from the beautiful new **promenade**, lined with bright bougainvillea and antique-style street furniture. This runs from the original town centre to the neighbouring resort of Jandía Playa. Look up to the cliff and you can see the big hotels where most people stay here.

The **old centre** of Morro Jable is reached by any of a number of narrow streets, which dive down to the sea across a dry riverbed.

OFF-ROAD DRIVING

While it is a fact that thousands of tourists do travel on the dirt tracks beyond Morro Jable in ordinary hire cars, it is not recommended to attempt this kind of off-road driving in anything other than a 4WD or Jeep-style vehicle. If it has recently rained heavily, don't even consider driving beyond Morro Jable in an ordinary car.

97

The South

> **GOOD RESTAURANTS**
> El Camello, La Pared (➤ 100)
> Marabú, Esquinzo (➤ 101)
> Fuerte action, Costa Calma (➤ 100)

Right on the seafront a dozen or so bars and restaurants cluster in an attractive lively jumble around a couple of small squares. At the heart of the main square is *El Viejo Vapor* (The Old Steamer), a real section of a steamship complete with funnel which used to house a restaurant but is, for the time being at least, vacant.

The port of Morro Jable, just south of the centre, is home to the local fishing fleet, scheduled ferry and jetfoil sailings to Gran Canaria and Tenerife, plus leisure excursions.
✚ 166 C1

28 Cofete

The road to Cofete begins promisingly, just south of Morro Jable, with brand new asphalt roads. Alas, these last barely 3km (2mi) and then it is another 24km (15mi) of teeth-rattling spine-jolting dirt-track driving. The last part of the journey, on little more than single-track hairpin bends with unprotected drops, is truly hair-raising! Slow down, use your horn on blind bends and be very careful. As you pass the highest point of the journey between the mountains of **Pico de la Zarza** (the island's highest peak) at 812m (2,663ft), and Pico de la Fraile at

A surfer's paradise: the beach of Playa Barca on the coast of Sotovento

At Your Leisure

686m (2,250ft), your reward is a view far along the north-west coast that will linger long in your memory. This is an awesome landscape unchanged in eons, on which man has made very little impression.

The ramshackle hamlet of Cofete with its café-restaurant is for many people the end of the line. Here they enjoy a well-earned cup of coffee, perhaps a meal and head back with a satisfying "been there, seen it" feeling. More intrepid explorers venture down to the magnificent but dangerous **beaches** and even further afield (➤ 89).

From the restaurant you can look out to the **mansion of Gustav Winter** (right), which sits isolated and brooding beneath the mountains. Low clouds often hang menacingly here and there is a real sense of drama. Little wonder that this has become the most talked about house on the island. Although it is only a short drive to the mansion do not attempt it unless you have a 4WD vehicle as the road is very bumpy indeed.

The 6m (20ft) long skeleton of a fin whale dangles from the ceiling in the Faro de Jandía **lighthouse to the west of** Morro Jable (Tue–Sat 10–6; free)
✚ 166 C2

Tourist office Jandía Playa
✚ 167 D1 ✉ CC Cosmo ☎ 928 540 776
🕒 Mon–Fri 8:45–2:45

Tourist office Morro Jable
✚ 166 C1 ✉ Morro Jable, on the beach just off the promenade 🕒 10–2:30

THE MYSTERY OF THE WINTER MANSION

Gustav Winter was born in Germany in 1893. He spent many years as an engineer in Spain and settled in Jandía in the early 1930s. In 1941 the authorities in Madrid officially assigned the whole peninsula of Jandía to the administration of Gustav Winter. Shortly after this it became a closed military zone. What subsequently happened at the Villa Winter is unknown but certainly during the war submarines were frequent visitors to Fuerteventura, refuelling here despite Spain's supposed neutrality.

Rumours buzz round to this day: Did Winter's property serve as a supply base for the German submarines during the Second World War? Was it from here that leading members of the Nazi party set off for South America at the end of the war? There is no evidence to support this claim but as the house has never been explored by outside parties it may still have tales to tell. During the 1950s, the villa was extended to produce its present form. In 1971, Don Gustavo died, and never revealed the mysteries of the mansion. There is no formal admission to the house but talk to the locals in Cofete and someone will be pleased to show you inside.

The South

Where to...
Eat and Drink

Prices
Expect to pay for a three-course meal for one, excluding drinks and service
€ under €15   €€ €15–€25   €€€ over €25

LA LAJITA

La Lajita Oasis Park €€
Oasis Park features three rustic restaurants decorated with greenery and rural bygones. The one by the main entrance backs onto exotic birdcages so their cries and calls make you feel as if you are eating in the jungle! (The other two are equally attractive and atmospheric but are only open to ticket holders.) It specialises in goat, so try the fried goat's cheese in breadcrumbs with *membrillo* (quince) jelly and then move onto goat stew, perhaps finishing with *frangollo* and ice cream.
🄴 167 F3 ✉ Carretera General de Jandía (FV-2 km 57.4) ☎ 928 161 135
🕐 11–5 (meals served from noon onwards)

LA PARED

El Camello €€€
This Andalusia-style hacienda is one of the most attractive restaurants in the whole of the island. There is a lovely garden and courtyard with tiled benches where you can snack on tapas, and the main dining area is straight from the pages of an interior design magazine, with pastel-washed walls, terracotta floors, tasteful chintzy soft furnishings and modern artworks. The menu might include *crab au gratin* with saffron sauce, tatar of salmon with potato pancakes as well as anglerfish medallions in vegetable and mustard sauce. Excellent wine list. Reservations recommended!
🄴 167 E3 ✉ Turn right on entering La Pared and follow the signs
☎ 928 549 090 🕐 Tue–Sun 1–11

Bahía La Pared €€
This beachside fish restaurant enjoys tremendous views and is very popular with locals and families, not least because there's a play area for children including a small pool with waterslides. The food is also excellent. If you're not sure which fish to choose ask the waiter for a recommendation. Book a table on the terrace, get here early evening and watch the sunset.
🄴 167 E3 ✉ Playas de la Pared
☎ 928 549 030 🕐 Daily noon–10

COSTA CALMA

Fuerte Action €–€€
Hang out with the surf dudes from all over Europe and beautiful people at this friendly relaxed trendy modern café. Surfing action plays on the screens but if that's not your thing you can easily escape on the terrace. Superior "fast foods" (spare ribs, chicken, pasta and home-made burgers), tapas, *bocadillos* (baguettes), a salad bar, good breakfasts, excellent coffee, juices, shakes and a mini-ice-cream parlour keep a broad range of customers coming back for more.
🄴 167 E3 ✉ CC El Palmeral (on main road next to petrol station) ☎ 928 875 996
🕐 Daily 8am–12:30am (last meals 10:30pm)

Where to...

Mediterran €€
This restaurant in the centre of the Las Abejas apartment complex (besides the Centro Comercial El Palmeral) is not the easiest place to find. As the name clearly indicates, the cuisine has a Mediterranean focus. Specialities include not only steaks and pasta but also lamb dishes, while gazpacho and minestrone are typical starters. Very relaxing atmosphere.
✚ 167 E3
✉ Calle Playa de la Jaqueta s/n
☎ 699 136 840
🕐 Daily from 5pm

Posada San Borondon I €€
This dark ancient-looking low-ceilinged wooden tavern bar is decorated with apple presses, huge barrels and earthenware jars and just drips with old-world atmosphere. Being in Costa Calma it's all fake of course, but no less enjoyable for that. The cheerful owner theatrically pours Sangria from a great height and dispenses free *croquetas* (croquettes) and other nibbles to a mixed lively cosmopolitan crowd who enjoy the live Spanish music (every night except Monday). There is a long and interesting menu of mainland and islands tapas (for example, Asturian beans, mushrooms in sherry, Lanzarote-style lentils).
✚ 167 E3 ✉ CC Sotavento
☎ 928 547 100 🕐 Daily 11am–1:30am

La Terraza del Gato €€
The Risco del Gato is Costa Calma's most individual and unusual hotel (➤ 103) and this classy modern white café-restaurant reflects its sense of minimalist style. From its international dishes you might choose chicken yakitori or breast of duck with port and grapes; from Spain there are lamb cutlets from Burgos, asparagus from Navarra, carpaccio with manchego cheese, a wide range of cold meats and sausages, plus Canarian favourites too. Snacks are very reasonably priced. Chill out on the terrace in a comfy cane chair and enjoy a sea view. Live music Thursday and Sunday.
✚ 167 E3 ✉ Calle Sicasumbre
☎ 928 547 030 🕐 Daily noon–10

ESQUINZO

Marabú €€
The family-run Marabú ("Feathers"), is tucked away between the main road and the beach of Esquinzo in a charming garden terrace courtyard in a modern development. The interior boasts many traditional elements yet is also light, modern and inviting. Chef Ralf Johmann brings many years of international experience to such dishes as chateaubriand, grilled parrot fish with Canarian potatoes, swordfish with a pepper crust and lamb specialities. Reservations recommended.
✚ 167 D2 ✉ Calle Fuente de Hija
☎ 928 544 098; www.e-marabu.com
🕐 Mon–Sat 1–11

JANDÍA PLAYA

Cervecería Olímpico €
This popular place is a clever mix of old-fashioned beer hall and 21st-century café, with floor to ceiling glass windows and a large attractive terrace where you can sit in comfy cane chairs looking across to the lighthouse. It has a wide selection of Spanish and German beers and an extensive range of other alcoholic drinks. At night the music is pumped up and it becomes a disco bar.
✚ 167 D1 ✉ Avenida del Saladar
☎ 928 166 012 🕐 Daily 10am–1am

Hong Kong €–€€
One of the best ethnic restaurants in the south, the authentic Chinese food at Hong Kong is ideal when you fancy a change from Canarian

The South

and Spanish cuisine. The chefs guarantee fresh fish and vegetables here so you may wish to add them to your choice of dishes, which in any case should include the house speciality, duck.
✚ 167 D1
✉ Cosmo Shopping Centre
☎ 928 540 827 ⓘ Daily 12–12

MORRO JABLE

Blue Marlin €–€€
Beautifully located by the water on the pedestrian promenade. Guests sit at the tables set with white linen either outside or in the light interior and enjoy fish in a salt crust or cheese fondue. The speciality of the house, fish grilled on a hot stone, is prepared by the guests themselves at the table. Different sauces and side dishes accompany the meat.
👶 There is a separate menu for children.
✚ 166 C1
✉ Avenida Tomás Grau Gurrea s/n
☎ 928 16 62 87 ⓘ Daily noon–11

Cofradía de Pescadores €
It's an experience to muck in with the local fishermen down at the port in their canteen bar, but actually more comfortable to sit outside where you can escape the TV and watch the boats. There's no frills and not a lot of choice – typically fish of the day, salad and potatoes, including the Canarian speciality of *papas arrugadas* – but quality and freshness is guaranteed, and, after all, if it's good enough for them…
✚ 166 C1
✉ Calle El Muelle
☎ 928 540 179 ⓘ Wed–Mon 8–5

Coronado €€€
One of the smartest and trendiest restaurants in the region. Coronado is ideal for a full meal or snack with a wide range of varying separate menus; Bar Lounge Classics (meals to share, including paella and fondues); Appetisers and Tapas; Soups and Salads; Steaks; Seafood. Make room for the Postres (desserts) Irresistible! The cuisine is of a very high standard and includes Thai, French, Italian and Spanish dishes. Extensive wine list with a choice of top wines round off the offer. Occasional live music and shows.
✚ 166 C1
✉ Calle El Sol, 14 ☎ 928 541 174; www.restaurantecoronado.com
ⓘ Thu–Tue 7pm–11pm

Posada San Borondon II €
Tucked away at the back of the ever-lively main square for restaurants, this dark single-storey colonial-style building hangs heavy with hams and garlic, agricultural implements and atmosphere. A menu of around 20 tapas is on offer, with live music most nights.
✚ 166 C1
✉ Peatonal La Piragua ("The Square")
☎ 928 541 428 ⓘ Daily noon–late

Saavedra Clavijo €€–€€€
This long-established restaurant is the most popular choice for fish in the old town. There is nearly always a buzz. Simply choose from the fresh fish display or ask the waiter for his recommendation.
✚ 166 C1
✉ Avenida Tomás Grau Gurrea
☎ 928 166 080 ⓘ Mon–Sat noon–late

Vesubio €–€€
Vesubio has a perfect people-watching location on the beach promenade just off the main square. Its menu wanders from island specials such as rabbit stew through 17 types of pizza and pasta respectively, or you could pick from the fresh fish display.
✚ 166 C1
✉ Avenida Tomás Grau Gurrea
☎ 928 540 391 ⓘ Daily 11–10:30

Where to...
Stay

Prices
Expect to pay per double room, per night
€ under €60   €€ €60–€90   €€€ €91–€120   €€€€ over €120

JANDÍA PLAYA

Faro Jandía €€€
Standing opposite the landmark *faro* (lighthouse) and set back from the main road, this 4-star hotel offers 214 spacious rooms to a mainly package-tour clientele. Nightly evening entertainment, three artificial grass tennis courts and the free use of a neighbouring Spa and Wellness Centre help to make this one of the resort's most popular hotels.

✚ 167 D1
✉ Jandía Playa Avenida del Saladar 17
☎ 928 545 035, www.hotelfarojandia.com

Iberostar Fuerteventura Palace €€€–€€€€
This new hotel is located on the main Jandía beach with bright pastel-coloured single-room studio apartments or one/two-bedroom apartments. Breakfast only, half-board and all-inclusive tariffs are available. The large complex has a large tennis court, one multi-purpose court several pools and a beautiful spa area. There are three 🛈 mini clubs for children and teenagers.

✚ 167 D1
✉ Urb. Las Gaviotas ☎ 928 540 444;
www.iberostarfuerteventurapalace.com

Robinson Club Jandía Playa €€€€
Established in 1970, this was the famous German club's first ever venture and the first club-resort complex of its kind on the island. Today its pioneering spirit might seem rather out of place amid the high rises and amusement arcades. It has been developed and extended, and has always had access to one of the best stretches of the Playa Mattoral. It offers a high standard of service and guests have a wide choice of different leisure and entertainment facilities.

The resort is renowned for its excellent sports and water sports programmes. Facilities include 10 tennis courts, 40 top-quality windsurf boards and rigs, nine Hobie Catamarans and a diving school. There is another Robinson Club nearby, at Esquinzo.

✚ 167 D1
✉ Jandía Playa, Avenida del Saladar
☎ 928 169 100; www.robinson.com

COSTA CALMA

Bungalows Risco del Gato €€€€
The Risco del Gato luxury suite hotel is jostled by high-rise neighbours but remains unequalled for style and class. Each extraordinary white bungalows which the architect intended to represent North African houses, comprises a conventionally housed bedroom, a round pod-like bathroom – featuring a large porthole window, Each suite has its own private patio and a hemispherical salon looking onto the gardens. There are two pools on different levels and the beautifully landscaped grounds provide a real feeling of space for its guests. The complex includes a new elegant Thai

The South

spa, a modern gym and a gourmet restaurant.
🏠 167 E3
✉ Calle Sicasumbre 2
☎ 928 547 175; www.vikhotels.com

Río Calma €€€€
Set high on a hill to the north, overlooking the whole resort, at first glance this building resembles a large church. Walk though its doors and you enter a huge mock-medieval space. A glass lift in the shape of a fairy-tale castle turret takes you to the accommodation area and now you are in colonial Spain, with pastel-washed colonnaded streets and houses. It could be the Gothic quarter of Barcelona or Toledo, and its glorious gardens front onto a cliff top. All 384 rooms have stunning sea views and enjoy every facility, including spa, gourmet restaurants, four pools, tennis courts, pitch and putt, mini-golf and a professional entertainment programme.
🏠 167 E3
✉ El Granillo
☎ 928 546 050; www.r2hotels.com

ESQUINZO

Jandía Princess €€€€
This large white landmark hotel is built in traditional Canarian style. There are 528 stylish bedrooms set in blocks that rise to three storeys high and look onto landscaped gardens, three large pools – one heated – and the beautiful and relatively quiet beach of Playa Butihondo.
🏠 167 D2
✉ Urb. Esquinzo Butihondo ☎ 928 544 089, 902 406 306; www.princess-hotels.com

MORRO JABLE

Hotel XQ El Palacete €€€
With just 54 rooms, of which two are junior suites, the El Palacete is one of the smaller hotel complexes on Fuerteventura. The two-floor complex overlooks the beach of Morro Jable – just across the pedestrian promenade and down some steps. There is a wonderful view of the sea and the resort from all the rooms. No loud entertainment programmes disturb guests looking for peace and quiet.
🏠 166 C1 ✉ Acantilado s/n
☎ 928 542 070, www.xqpalacete.com

PLAYA BARCA

Club Aldiana €€€€
Renowned for its extensive sports, spa and wellness facilities, the German-run Club Aldiana is one of the pioneers of this region, arriving here in the late 1970s. It is set in attractive grounds that tumble down to a beautiful stretch of beach where there is a diving school, and a fish restaurant. Most of its bungalows are fairly simple though there are a handful of newer luxury accommodations too.
🏠 167 E2
✉ Playa de Jandía
☎ 928 169 870; www.aldiana.de

Meliá Gorriones €€€–€€€€
From an architectural point of view, there are doubtless nicer looking hotels on Fuerteventura, but the hotel's location on Playa Barca, one of the island's most famous beaches, is absolutely phenomenal. Not surprisingly, the rooms at the Gorriones are always in demand. Surfers love the place. Its facilities are excellent, and the extensive mature grounds include four pools, one tennis court, a health centre and a gym. The famous Pro Centre René Egli Windsurf School (➤ 106) is also based here. The first row of Casas del Mar apartments in the recently extended building complex offer great comfort and wonderful views.
🏠 167 E2 ✉ Playa Barca
☎ 928 547 025; www.solmelia.com

Where to... Shop

JANDÍA PLAYA

Most of the south's shopping opportunities are confined to the shopping centres of Jandía Playa and Costa Calma. The former is limited to cheap souvenirs, jewellers, perfume shops, duty-free electronics shops and "shoe bazaars" where you are expected to haggle over the price of footwear.

The **CC Cosmo** (the last one on the main road heading to Morro Jable) is the best of the bunch, with its **Juwelier Continental** featuring brand names.

The island's weekly market sets out its stalls next door to the Cosmo every Thursday and at Costa Calma on Sunday morning.

COSTA CALMA

Costa Calma has more shopping centres than Jandía Playa though few of these offer little that is different or original. The best is the **El Palmeral**, on the main road by the filling station.

If you want to see what the well-heeled surf dude is wearing then pop into **Fuerte Action**, which has some of the most stylish surf clothes and accessories on the island. This brand is the brainchild of René Egli, who owns a water sports centre (▶ 106), so everything here is designed to be functional as well as fashionable. It's not cheap but it is high quality.

Next door **Hodge Podge** also ha some good surfing gear.

Inside the shopping centre, **Mystic** is good for aloe vera products and a small range of handicrafts. Based on a similar philosophy of natural products and handicrafts, The Earth Collection is worth a browse for island-sourced gifts and souvenirs.

The jewellery at **First One**, here prices range from pocket money to serious euros, is among the best on the entire island. (They also have a branch in the LTI Esquinzo Beach Hotel at Urb. Esquinzo Butihondo.)

Fuerte Cabrito sells clothes and accessories stylishly branded with the ubiquitous Fuerte goat logo (branches also in Morro Jable and Costa Calma).

If you would like some Canarian flowers for the table at home then pop into Strelitzias at the **Centro Commercial Costa Calma** and they will pack these specially to be stowed in the aircraft hold.

MORRO JABLE

The old part of Morro Jable has only a few shops of interest. Next to the square that holds the cafés, bars and restaurants, on Calle Nuestra Señora del Carmen, you will find **Fuerte Cabrito**.

Situated just above the old town of Morro Jable is the very well-stocked **Supermercado Padilla**. Here, self-caterers will find a good selection of fresh products and cheese from Fuerteventura. The Padilla chain also has branches in, for instance, Jandía Playa (Centro Commercial Ventura) and Costa Calma (Centro Commercial Bahía Calma).

LA LAJITA OASIS PARK

The shop at La Lajita Oasis Park sells a wide range of home accessories and unusual gifts. It's almost worth stopping just to look in the shop.

The South

Where to... Go Out

NIGHTLIFE

Most of the nightlife in this part of the island is confined to the large hotels and resort club complexes. Jandía Playa is the liveliest place with a number of disco bars. On summer weekends try the Discothek Stella at the **Stella Canaris Hotel**, the **Disco Pub Tequila** in the CC Atlantico or the **Cervecería Olímpico** on the seafront.

Costa Calma, true to its name, is generally quiet after dark though you might like to try the **PMP** disco-pub at the CC Cañada del Río, or in **Bar Teide** at the Sotavento Beach Club, Avenida Jahn Reisen.

Fuerte Action (▶ 100) is generally lively. On the other side of the road in Costa Calma, the **San Borondon I** (▶ 101) is not only a good place to eat but has live music.

WATER SPORTS

The **Pro Centre René Egli**, based at Sotavento Beach, is one of Europe's top centres for windsurfing. It is an excellent venue for just getting started or for polishing up your technique. Their expert coaches come from all over the world.

Water sports facilities and instruction is highly rated at the club holiday village complexes of **Club Aldiana** (▶ 104) though these are only open to guests.

For diving try the **Sotavento Beach Club** at Costa Calma (tel: 928 547 060), or the **Felix Barakuda Club** at Jandía Playa (tel: 928 541 418; www.tauchen-fuerteventura.com). On the rugged west coast, **La Pared** has become an El Dorado for surfers. Several schools there offer surf camps and expert tuition, for example **Waveguru** (tel: 619 804 447, www.waveguru.de) and **Adrenalin Surfschool** (tel: 928 949 034, www.adrenalin-surfschool.com).

OTHER SPORTS

Walking holidays on Fuerteventura are becoming increasingly popular and there are now many marked routes even on the Jandía isthmus. A particular favourite is the trail from Morro Jable via a mountain pass to Cofete. Near the lighthouse in the little village of El Puertito, a path leads to the cliffs of Caleta Madera or to Punta Pesebre. **Time for Nature** (tel: 928 872 545, www.timefornature.de) organises guided tours, also to other parts of the island and on Lobos.

Tennis Matchpoint (www.matchpoint-world.de) is an enterprising company with seven German tennis coaches (English spoken) who offer tuition and put you together with players of similar ability to make up tournaments which are staged on the artificial grass courts at ten of the south's leading hotels.

EXCURSIONS

Numerous deep-sea and big-game fishing trips depart from Morro Jable harbour and if you are in a group it might be worth chartering your own yacht for the day. The *Magic Cat* catamaran sails from Morro Jable (tel: 619 406 904).

If you would like to look beneath the waves the 🆔 **Subcat** (tel: 900 507 006), a twin-hulled submarine also based at Morro Jable will take you 30m (100ft) down. Lasting a good hour, the submarine trip is not cheap at €60 per person.

Lanzarote

Finding Your Feet	108
Getting Your Bearings	110
The Perfect Day	112
Top 10	114
Don't Miss	118
At Your Leisure	120
Where to…	124

☀ Little Treats

Architectural grandeur
In the Oasis de Nazaret near Teguise, the **Lag-O-Mar** restaurant (➤ 125) invites you to enjoy its spectacular setting in an old volcanic stone quarry.

Lanzarote's wild north coast
The rolling waves of **Playa de Famara** north of Teguise (➤ 119) are not only popular with surfers.

Elegant harbour
Just west of Puerto del Carmen (➤ 123), you can stroll past the yachts in **Puerto Calero's marina**.

Lanzarote

Finding Your Feet

Getting to Lanzarote
Express boat and catamaran services run from Corralejo to Playa Blanca at the southern tip of Lanzarote and to Puerto del Carmen on the southern coastline.

Services to Playa Blanca
- The **catamaran**, operated by Fred Olsen, carries vehicles and foot passengers and takes just 20 minutes to cross the water. The first catamaran to Playa Blanca leaves Corralejo at 7:45am (except at weekends when it is 9am). The last departure from Playa Blanca is at 6pm. Tel: 902 100 107; www.fredolsen.es.
- The *Volcán de Tindaya*, operated by Naviera Armas, also carries vehicles and foot passengers but takes 30 minutes. The first **boat** to Playa Blanca leaves Corralejo at 8am and the last departure from Playa Blanca is at 7pm. Tel: 902 456 500; www.navieraarmas.com.
- From Playa Blanca a free **bus** takes passengers to Puerto del Carmen (stopping at the Centro Comercial Biosfera Plaza – shopping centre) and then on to the centre of Arrecife. The total journey takes just 45 minutes.

CÉSAR MANRIQUE
The most famous son of Lanzarote is the talented artist and landscape architect César Manrique (1919–92). He not only designed unique attractions, he successfully pushed through strict regulations to safeguard the character of the island. Despite Manrique's endeavours, however, Lanzarote has not totally escaped the negative consequences of mass tourism.

When to visit
Several restaurants close on Monday. If you are visiting Teguise avoid Saturday and note Sunday is market day (► 42).

Sightseeing on Lanzarote
For sightseeing around the island take your own hire car from Fuerteventura on the ferry to Playa Blanca. In recent years this resort has shown tremendous growth and now stretches along the south coast for several kilometres and quite a way inland as well. A very beautiful pedestrian promenade connects the coves, some of which are man-made.

If you don't already have a hire car on Fuerteventura, then you can pick one up from the Cabrera Medina office at the port, or from one of the other local car hire companies in the adjacent shopping centre. Cabrera Medina (tel: 928 822 900; www.cabreramedina.com) is usually more expensive than Lanzarote's local operators, but for one day's hire this is probably not a significant amount.

If you don't want to hire a car but still wish to go sightseeing then you can catch a taxi from the port. A full island day tour costs around €160.

Tourist information offices
The information office at Playa Blanca is a ten-minute walk from the port. The office at Puerto del Carmen is on the beach, a good half-hour's walk away from the port.

🛈 www.turismolanzarote.com 🕓 Mon–Fri 10am–5pm, closing at 4pm Jul, Aug, Sep.
➕ Playa Blanca ✉ Calle Limones ☎ 928 519 018
➕ Puerto del Carmen ✉ Avenida de las Playas ☎ 928 513 351

Finding Your Feet

WHICH WINE?
Wines from Lanzarote bear a protected appellation of origin (Denominación de Origen, D.O.) on their label. The main wine-growing area is the La Geria region, which is where the market leader **El Grifo** (www.elgrifo.com) also has large vineyards. Over the years, the heavy Malvasia-based wine has increasingly lost ground to lighter wines, especially the dry *(seco)* and semi-dry *(semi seco)* white and red wines made from the Listán blanco, Listán negro, Negramol and Moscatel grape varieties.

In the bodegas on the wine trail from La Geria, you can try different vintages as you look out at the barren lava fields in which vines are grown using a very sophisticated cultivation system.

Shopping

In general, goods on Lanzarote differ little from those on Fuerteventura, though there is more choice and, more often than not, better quality.

Lanzarote has three unique "products": its volcanoes, its wines, and a gentleman named César Manrique (▶ info box on the left). There are souvenirs of all these.

All the Manrique-inspired visitor attractions sell stylish T-shirts, accessories, jewellery, posters and other goods designed by or associated with the great man. **Fundación César Manrique** shops, carrying a wider range of goods, can be found at Puerto del Carmen, Playa Blanca, Arrecife and Teguise.

The **artisans** of Lanzarote produce some beautiful jewellery – particularly notable are those pieces that incorporate black lava and green olivine, often combined in necklaces. Olivine is the island's most valuable natural mineral, a semi-precious stone that is produced by volcanic forces.

Lanzarote

Getting Your Bearings

A drive through the countryside on Lanzarote is a picture-book experience: black lava fields contrast with white fincas with a date palm or two often providing a green highlight. Compared with Fuerteventura, the different architectural style is clearly visible.

A few kilometres north of the man-made resort of Playa Blanca lies Yaiza, a well-kept showcase village and the gateway to the stunning Parque Nacional de Timanfaya (national park). This was the epicentre of the massive volcanic eruptions of 1730–36 that gave the island's landscape much of the character seen today, and the park is a must-see on any visit to the island, however short.

South of the national park is Lanzarote's biggest resort, Puerto del Carmen. Like Corralejo it retains its original fishing port alongside a long beachfront, popular with tourists. Just west is Arrecife, the capital, with some fine shops, an interesting mix of old and new buildings, a picturesque lagoon and a world-renowned modern art collection.

Due north at Tahiche, built into volcanic caves, is the incredible former home of the island hero and driving force César Manrique (➤ 108). Just north of this is the old capital of Teguise, Lanzarote's historical *tour de force*, a beautifully preserved collection of houses and palazzos (palaces) which date back to the 15th century. Further north and east lies the island's most famous Manrique attractions: the Jameos del Agua, the Jardín de Cactus and the Mirador del Río, as well as Haría, the beautiful "Village of 1000 Palms".

Near El Golfo is a collapsed volcano crater, in which there is now a bright green lagoon

Getting Your Bearings

TOP 10
⭐ Parque Nacional de Timanfaya ➤ 114
⭐ Jameos del Agua ➤ 116

Don't Miss
㉙ Teguise ➤ 118

At Your Leisure
㉚ El Golfo ➤ 120
㉛ La Geria ➤ 120
㉜ Fundación César Manrique ➤ 120
㉝ Haría ➤ 121
㉞ Mirador del Río ➤ 121
㉟ Cueva de los Verdes ➤ 122
㊱ Jardín de Cactus ➤ 122
㊲ Arrecife ➤ 123
㊳ Puerto del Carmen ➤ 123

Perfect Days in...

Lanzarote

The Perfect Day

The following recommended route is based on the assumption that you will be taking your hire car to Lanzarote. This suggested itinerary offers a good way to visit some of the most interesting sights in the south of the island in just three days. For more information see the main entries (➤ 114–123).

Morning

Catch the first ferry and arrive in Lanzarote around 7:30am. Head towards Yaiza on the LZ2 and after 10km (6mi) turn left to visit **30 El Golfo** (➤ 120). From here drive towards Yaiza, rejoin the LZ2 and turn left after 1–2km (0.6–1mi) towards the ⭐**Parque Nacional de Timanfaya** (photo right, ➤ 114; opens 9am). Have a coffee, watch the volcanic effects demonstrated by the ranger and take the 35-minute bus tour (these depart every few minutes).

Return towards Yaiza, turn left onto the LZ2 and after 1km (0.6mi) turn left onto the LZ30, a very picturesque road which cuts through the heart of **31 La Geria** (➤ 120), Lanzarote's wine region (left). Approximately 100m after the landmark Bodega Geria, keep your eyes peeled for the **Bodega El Chupadero** (➤ 125). This is a beautiful location and, depending on your day's plan and rate of progress, is a great place to stop for a coffee or an early lunch.

The LZ30 continues for another 13km (8mi) to the Monumento al Campesino, a stunning white abstract statue by César Manrique that marks the centre of the island. Its bodega is another good snack lunch option.

The Perfect Day

Afternoon

Continue on the same road to
29 Teguise, the colonial island capital (➤ 118). Visit the Palacio Herrea and mooch around the cobbled squares and alleyways admiring the architecture and some of the beautiful shops inside the lovingly restored old houses. Try to leave here by 2pm. Just past the Castillo de Santa Barbara, take the turn right to Teseguite and after 6km (4mi) turn left onto the LZ1. After 1km (0.6mi) take the signpost right to Guatiza and after another 3km (2mi) is the
36 Jardín de Cactus (➤ 122), César Manrique's magnificent piece of botanic modern art. There is a lovely café here but try to get back on the road by 3pm. Continue driving north, rejoining the LZ1 after 1–2km (0.5–1mi). After another 3km (2mi) fork off right to the **10 Jameos del Agua** (➤ 116), regarded by many as Manrique's tour de force. It takes around an hour to explore this at a leisurely pace. Aim to leave by 4:15pm. Return south along the LZ1 towards
37 Arrecife (photo left, ➤ 123), pick up the ring road *(circunvalacion)* then Tias and Yaiza signs, and this will take you back to Yaiza on fast roads in around one hour. This should give you just enough time for a quick meal at one of the fish restaurants in Arrieta, before returning on the dual carriageway to the harbour at Playa Blanca.

Lanzarote

⭐ Parque Nacional de Timanfaya

The Timanfaya National Park, or Montañas del Fuego (Fire Mountains) as this area is also called, is one of the Earth's spectacular landscapes. Earth, however, will probably be the farthest place from your mind as you gaze upon this scorched and contorted terrain. Its brooding craters and blasted badlands resemble a distant planet.

Timanfaya was mostly created between 1730 and 1736 in a series of 26 volcanic eruptions, which devastated around a quarter of the island and buried 11 villages. Due to the "slow burn" nature of the volcanic action on Lanzarote there was plenty of time for evacuation and no one is reported to have lost their life.

On a camel or a bus

It is best to approach from the south; the volcanic debris begins just north of Yaiza and an impish César Manrique designed devil welcomes you to the park. It is forbidden to leave your vehicle and walk among the *malpais* (literally, badlands), unless supervised by a qualified guide (▶ 115 box), and the first parking point is at the **Echadero de los Camellos** ("Camel Park"). This can be a chaotic spot, though, as tour buses stop here to let off passengers who want to queue for dromedaries to take them on the short 🐪 **camel ride** up and down the mountainside. It's worth a look but the most spectacular part of the park is still to come.

Inhabitants refer to this unforgettable stretch of countryside as the Malpais, literally the "badlands"

The Earth's natural geothermal heat cooks the meat on this barbecue

Once past the pay booth you must drive the short way into the park and leave your car next to the Visitor Centre. Here a park ranger demonstrates that the volcano beneath your feet is still very much alive; a bucket of water is emptied into a tube into the ground and transformed into a scalding geyser; a dry bush is dropped into a fissure and promptly ignites and in the manner of a practical joke, you may be invited to hold a handful of (hot) earth that the ranger scoops from the ground.

Also from here coaches depart more or less continuously on the **Ruta de los Volcanes** (Route of the Volcanoes) tour. This is an unforgettable 35-minute trip taking in the highlights of the central part of the park with a short commentary in different languages, accompanied by evocative mood music and sounds.

TAKING A BREAK

The restaurant enjoys 360-degree views from large glass panels and the food, which you can see barbecuing on a large **grill above the heat of the volcano**, is very good quality, tel: 928 173 105 for reservations. Restaurant noon–3:30, café/bar 9–4:45.

✠ 168 B2/3
☎ 928 173 789; www.centrosturisticos.com
🕐 Daily 9–5:45, Summer until 6:45, last coach tour 5/6pm 💶 €9

INSIDER INFO

- Don't worry about whether to watch the **geothermal displays** before or after the coach trip as they are demonstrated more or less continuously throughout the day.
- There are two **walking tours** that enter the Parque National de Timanfaya. One is free, led by park rangers and departs from the Mancha Blanca Visitor Centre on Monday, Wednesday and Friday (you must book in advance, tel: 928 840 839; www.reservasparquesnacionales.com). The tour by Canary Trekking, a company formed by ex-rangers, is longer and quite expensive but excellent (tel: 609 537 684; www.canarytrekking.com).
- If you have never **ridden a camel** before then Timanfaya is certainly a novel place to start, but if it's really busy don't worry about giving it a miss – there's plenty more to see.

Lanzarote

⭐10 Jameos del Agua

Regarded by many as César Manrique's most spectacular creation, the Jameos del Agua was also his first tourist centre on the island. A *jameo* ("ha-may-oh") is created when superheated volcanic gas shoots through solid rock to form a tube or cave – the *jameo* itself is that part of the tube whose roof has collapsed to let in light. Here, two *jameos* and a lava canal running between them have been turned into a fantasy grotto.

You descend into the first *jameo* to find a cool dark café-bar area, filled with lush tropical plants. New Age mood music may be playing. As your eyes adjust you can see little niches and alcoves that come into their own at night when it becomes a restaurant – occasional musical events are staged here. This is joined to a cave with a lake. Peer closely and you will see that the still water is populated by hundreds of tiny almost fluorescent white spider-like albino crabs. They once lived deep in the ocean but were stranded here long ago and this is the only place in the world where they are now found.

One of the jameos is now a swimming pool in an idyllic setting

Pool and volcano houses

As you emerge up from the darkness there is a shock in store. The second *jameo* is a South Seas-style swimming **pool**, bright blue with a blinding white "beach" (painted stone), picturesque black and grey rocks and of course a tall palm tree set at a picture-postcard angle over the pool. At the far end of the pool the final cave is home to an auditorium with near-perfect acoustics that is used for concerts and folklore shows.

Jameos del Agua

Enjoy the special atmosphere in this volcanic cave

Ascend the steps and you will find a series of more "conventional" rooms housing the **Casas de los Volcanes** (Volcano Houses) exhibition area and a research centre. This is an excellent hands-on introduction to the world of volcanoes and will answer just about any question on vulcanology in Lanzarote, the Canary Islands or indeed the world.

Insider Tip

TAKING A BREAK

There is a bar at either end of your visit. The first may be a little too dark for some people. If so, go to the one up the steps above the swimming pool. Both sells snacks and are rather expensive.

169 F4 ☎ 928 848 020; www.centrosturisticos.com
🕐 Daily 10–6:30, also Sat 7:30pm–10pm €9

Restaurant
☎ 928 848 024 🕐 Tue–Sat 11–4:30, also Tue, Sat 7:30pm–11:30pm €€€

INSIDER INFO

- If you have time then visit the **Cueva de los Verdes**, which is part of the same underground network – the entrance is just a few hundred metres away (▶ 122). It is interesting to compare this "unadorned" version with Manrique's fantasy world.
- In Arrieta **El Amanacer** (▶ 125) invites you to fish and seafood.

Insider Tip

Lanzarote

🔴29 Teguise

Founded in the 15th century, Teguise is the oldest town on Lanzarote. It was the conquistadors' capital and remained so until 1852. Today many of its whitewashed colonial-style houses have been lovingly restored and are home to top-quality restaurants and shops.

Teguise is small, with no modern sprawl attached and very little traffic in its narrow streets. It only takes 10 to 15 minutes to walk from one end of the town to the other so this is an ideal place for strolling.

For six days of the week Teguise slumbers, but on Sunday thousands of visitors flock here to its touristy **market**, which takes over the town centre. The German and English market stands selling national food are not particularly popular. Folklore dancers and musicians perform in the main square, which is dominated by the handsome **Iglesia de Nuestra Señora de Guadalupe**. However, the interior, damaged by a fire in 1909, was poorly restored and is disappointing.

On the square you can visit the **Palacio Spínola**, built from 1730–80, now the **Timple Museum** *(casa-museo)*, and you can also look inside the Caja Canarias bank (closed on Sunday), which was once the *cilla* or church grain store, built in 1680. Next to the main square the Plaza de Julio 18 is lined with historic buildings now home to shops and restaurants. Just off the square there is a very picturesque snowy white-topped building with a characteristic Canarian balcony. This is the 17th-century **Casa Cuartel**, formerly an army barracks.

The popular market takes place every Sunday

Teguise

Sacred art

One of the town's two convents has also found a new role. The 18th-century **Convento de Santo Domingo** houses modern art exhibitions, while the handsome 16th-century **Convento de San Francisco** is now a museum of sacred art. Between the latter and the church, don't miss the **Palacio del Marqués**, on Calle Marqués de Herrera y Rojas. Built in 1455, it is the oldest building in town and is now home to a tapas bar.

Iglesia de Nuestra Señora de Guadalupe towers over Teguise

TAKING A BREAK

You are spoiled for choice: The **Bodega Santa Barbara** (Calle Cruz 5; tel: 928 845 200 is particularly good or opt for the **Bodeguita del Medio** (➤ 125).

🗺 169 D3 🌐 www.turismoteguise.org

Convento de Santo Domingo
✉ Calle de Santo Domingo ☎ 928 845 001
🕐 Sun–Fri 10–3 💰 Free

Palacio Spínola
✉ Plaza de la Constitution ☎ 928 845 181
🕐 Sun–Fri 9–4 (Jul, Aug, Sep closes one hour earlier)

Palacio del Marqués
✉ Calle Marqués de Herrera y Rojas ☎ 609 475 043
🕐 Mon–Sat 9–4:30, Sun 9–3:30

Castillo de Santa Barbara
✉ 1km (0.5mi) north east of Teguise
☎ 928 845 001 🕐 Mon–Fri 10–3:30, Sat 10:30–2:30 💰 €3

INSIDER INFO

- Come on a **Sunday** for the atmosphere but do visit the shops (they are all open) rather than just patronising the market stalls.
- The 16th-century **Castillo de Santa Barbara**, on the hill above Teguise, houses a fascinating and quite poignant 🎭 **pirate museum**. Even if you don't go in, there are wonderful views.
- The small village of Caleta de Famara is approximately 12 km (7.5 mi) north of Teguise. This is where you will find Lanzarote's longest beach, the **Playa de Famara**. *Insider Tip*

Lanzarote

At Your Leisure

30 El Golfo
Next to the little white fishing village of El Golfo is one of the island's most curious coastal and volcanic landscapes. Arriving from the south there are two approaches. The first is signposted "Charco de los Clicos" and takes you past a remarkably eroded and striated cliff to a black lava beach and a spectacular rock outcrop. At the back of the beach, half of the El Golfo volcano has fallen away to create an amphitheatre rich in reds and orange hues. The star sight is the enclosed lagoon, which has a deep emerald green colour, probably caused by algae, though another theory is that it may also be due to the presence of the semi-precious stone olivine.

The best view of the lagoon is actually from above, on the elevated walkway accessed from the village (follow the signpost to El Golfo).
✚ 168 B2

31 La Geria
Lanzarote's wine-growing region is like no other in the world. Vines are planted in depressions in order that they can delve deep beneath the layer of volcanic ash down to the soil. Each is surrounded by a horseshoe-shaped dry stone wall, about a metre high, which helps the lava covering the crop to retain what little moisture there is and protects it from the wind. The sight of thousands of these *zocos*, as they are known, against the dark lava landscape is quite stunning. The area can be seen while travelling the LZ30 from Uga to the Monumento al Campesino and you may well wish to stop in some of the many bodegas en route to sample the wine. *Inside Tip*
✚ 168 C2

32 Fundación César Manrique (Taro de Tahiche/Manrique's House)
The Fundación César Manrique promotes artistic environmental and cultural activities and was created by the great man himself (➤ 108) in 1982. It is based at the remarkable home of Manrique *Tip* called Taro de Tahiche. Like Jameos del Agua (➤ 116), which it pre-dates, it is built on the site of a lava flow and *jameos* (volcanic bubbles) are a fundamental part of its design. It holds a contemporary art collection, including many works by

---

INSIDER INFO

■ **Unusual features** on the south-west coast:
El Golfo: a bright green lagoon and half a volcano (➤ above); Los Hervideros: caves and grottos where the sea bubbles and boils; Salinas de Janubio: Lanzarote's largest salt flats, still in action today

■ **Magical underground tours**
Taro de Tahiche: César Manrique's ingenious home (➤ 120); Jameos del Agua: the ultimate fantasy grotto (➤ 116–117); Cueva de los Verdes: where boiling lava once burrowed its way through the earth (➤ 122)

■ **Wonderful views**
Mirador del Río (➤ 121), one of the most spectacular lookout points for miles, and Castillo de Santa Barbara, Teguise (➤ 119)

At Your Leisure

A sophisticated cultivation technique ensures that the vines in La Geria have enough water

Manrique, but the star exhibit is the home itself.
🗺 169 E2 ✉ Tahiche
☎ 928 843 138; www.fcmanrique.org
🕐 Daily 10–6 💶 €8

33 Haría
This charming little pristine town of white cube-like houses sits in the beautiful "Valley of 1000 Palms" and inevitably invites comparison with a North African oasis. A short pedestrianised tree-lined avenue, at its best on Saturday when the Craft Market stalls are out, leads to the church and the adjacent **Museo de Arte Sacro** (Sacred Art Museum). Haría is a magnet for the art and crafts community and has some very good shops.
🗺 169 E4 ✉ Museo de Arte Sacro
☎ 928 835 011
🕐 Mon–Sat 9–3 💶 €1.50

34 Mirador del Río *Insider Tip*
A *mirador* is a lookout point and this one, originally a gun battery, is probably the most spectacular in the whole archipelago. It was carefully designed by César Manrique so that neither the entrance nor the curving corridor which takes you into the main room give you any idea what is coming next – which is a wide-angle almost aerial view through full-length windows of the **Isla la Graciosa** and the bright blue straits of El Río. You can go outside to appreciate the *mirador*'s location, set into the side of a jaw-dropping sheer cliff face that plummets 450m (1476ft) to the sea.
🗺 169 E4 ℹ www.centrosturisticos.com
🕐 Daily 10–5:45 💶 €4.50

121

Lanzarote

35 Cueva de los Verdes

The Volcán de la Corona that created the Jameos del Agua (➤ 116) also created the Cueva de los Verdes (The Green's Cave). It takes its name from a family who once lived here and in the 16th and 17th centuries was used by the islanders as a refuge from pirates and slave traders. A guided tour takes you on a spectacular 2km (1mi) journey through this labyrinth. Unlike the Jameos del Agua it has not been landscaped but it is artfully lit and the tour ends with a memorable optical illusion.

🗺 169 E4
☎ 928 848 484; www.centrosturisticos.com
⏰ Daily 10–6 (last entry 5) 💶 €9

COCHINEAL
Next to the Jardín de Cactus parking area an old man demonstrates just why so many cacti are grown in this part of the island. They attract a parasitic bug which when dried and crushed gives cochineal, a bright red colouring used in the food and drink industry, most notably for Campari.

36 Jardín de Cactus

Even the least horticulturally inclined visitor will find this an amazing landscape. Crammed in to the semi-natural amphitheatre of a former quarry are 10,000 cacti of all shapes (spot the fire hydrants, cauliflower ears, giant cucumbers, starfish, snakes), all sizes, and every shade of green plus yellow and even purple. Dalí-esque fingers of volcanic rock and a windmill complete the surreal scene. It was one of Manrique's last works and also one of his favourites.

🗺 169 E3 ✉ Between Guatiza and Mala
☎ 928 529 397; www.centrosturisticos.com
⏰ Daily 10–6 (last admission 5:45) 💶 €5.50

Over 10,000 cacti in every imaginable colour and size flourish in the Jardín de Cactus

It is fun going for a walk by the sea in Arrecife

37 Arrecife

Once regarded as a last resort, rainy-day shopping option, the capital of the island has smartened itself up immeasurably over the last few years and is now a very rewarding excursion whatever the weather. Its promenade is lined with tropical gardens and its picture-book bandstand has been smartly renovated. A very pleasant **craft market** comes here every Wednesday. On the landside are a row of restored houses spanning several styles and centuries while a causeway leads to the **Castillo de San Gabriel**, built in 1590. Formerly home to a small archaeological museum it is now open for exhibitions only.

Take a stroll along the pedestrianised shopping street and turn off to find the picturesque **Iglesia de San Ginés**, beautifully restored to its 18th-century glory. Behind here the **Charco (lagoon) of San Ginés** is a peaceful spot for a walk, with its fishing boats at anchor and choice of bars and restaurants around the lagoon.

Further on, a short walk just past the port, is the capital's main visitor attraction, the **Castillo de San José**, built in the late 18th century and restored by César Manrique to hold the internationally acclaimed **Museo Internacional de Arte Contemporáneo** (International Museum of Contemporary Art). Works rotate but you may spot pieces by Picasso or Miró and certainly a Manrique or two. The contrast between the ancient dark stones and the vibrant modern artworks is rarely less than impressive. The castle is also home to one of the island's finest restaurants (➤ 124).
🞤 169 D2   ℹ️ www.centrosturisticos.com

Museo Internacional de Arte Contemporáneo
✉️ Castillo de San José, Carretera de Puerto Naos ☎ 928 812 321
🕙 Daily 10–8   💶 €4

38 Puerto del Carmen

Puerto del Carmen is Lanzarote's main resort. Its main strip, the Avenida de las Playas, is lined with scores of bars, restaurants and nightspots and its beaches stretch half way to Arrecife. There are more than enough shops and eating options here to keep you happy. The most attractive part of the town is around the port.
🞤 168 C2

Lanzarote

Where to...
Eat and Drink

Prices
Expect to pay for a three-course meal for one, excluding drinks and service
€ under €15   €€ €15–€25   €€€ over €25

PUERTO DEL CARMEN

Bodega €€–€€€
Take your pick from the cosy tapas bar, or the main restaurant area, open to the street, with a mouth-watering display of meats. Steaks and grills are the restaurant speciality though you'll be equally welcome in the tapas bar for a glass of the very good house wine and perhaps some scrambled eggs with king prawns or fried goats' cheese with cranberries. Conveniently located in the heart of the old town, just above the port.
✚ 168 C2   ✉ Calle Roque Nuiblo 3
☎ 928 512 953   ⏰ Daily 1–midnight

Bodegón El Sardinero €€–€€€
One of the best places for fish in the Old Town, El Sardinero offers a choice of two dining experiences. The larger, formal branch is in the lower square, close to where the boats dock. Its smart dining room is upstairs, above a popular bar, and has good views onto the port. A few metres uphill, at the start of the restaurants with balconies that look down onto the square, you will find its other branch: small, cosy with red-gingham tablecloths.
✚ 168 C2   ✉ Calle Tenerife ("upper" restaurant)   ☎ 928 512 128   ⏰ Noon–11
✉ Dockside restaurant
☎ 928 511 847   ⏰ Noon–11

La Lonja €€
Located in the old town district directly by the harbour, La Lonja used to be Puerto del Carmen's fish market, today it is a lively restaurant. In the usually well frequented bar on the ground floor, you can drink a beer or a glass of local wine as you nibble on a tapa, or savour a piece of fish in the main restaurant.
✚ 168 C1   ✉ Calle Varadero s/n
☎ 928 511 377   ⏰ Daily noon–midnight

ARRECIFE

Castillo de San José €€–€€€   *Inside Tip*
This César Manrique-designed restaurant has a wooden floor, black-plastic 1960s-style seats and floor-to-ceiling windows giving wonderful sea views. Start with monkfish and salmon carpaccio, then try *cherne* (stone bass) with king prawns or thyme, or a flambéed steak, and finish with *gofio* ice cream. Cool jazz music complements the sophisticated calm atmosphere.
✚ 169 D2   ✉ Carretera de Puerto Naos
☎ 928 812 321
⏰ 1–3:45, 7:30–11 (bar open 11am–midnight)

Emmax €€
Set in a typical single-storey Canarian house, but with a modern light stylish interior, this restaurant-café – opened in 2007 – is already a local favourite. The choice changes daily. The cooking is Italian-influenced modern Canarian. Do try the black pasta with prawns in an orange sauce if available, sea bass is another good choice (there are always fresh fish options), and the house salad is excellent.
✚ 169 D2   ✉ Avenida Playa Honda 21
☎ 928 820 917   ⏰ Wed–Mon noon–midnight

At Your Leisure

TEGUISE

Bodeguita del Medio €–€€
This atmospheric little dark hole-in-the-wall tapas bar, set in an historic building, usually spills out onto the pavement where its menu is etched onto its wooden tables. You can also buy local delicacies from the shop inside.

🗺 169 D3 ✉ Plaza Clavijo y Fajardo 5
☎ 928 845 680
🕐 Mon–Fri noon–9, Sat–Sun noon–4

Lag-O-Mar €€–€€€ *Insider Tip*
In the little village of Oasis de Nazaret not far south of Teguise, the Lag-O-Mar serves Mediterranean and local dishes in a spectacular stone quarry setting. The surroundings are unforgettable; the volcanic rock shines beautifully as the sun sets.

🗺 169 D3 ✉ C/Los Loros, 2, Nazaret
☎ 928 845 665; www.lag-o-mar.com
🕐 Tue–Sat noon–midnight, Sun noon–6

ARRIETA

El Amanacer €€
If you are lucky, you will find a spot on the terrace overlooking the sea. This popular restaurant has a large selection of fresh fish and seafood dishes. The *Cherne* (sea bass) is always good and – like the other fish dishes – is served in the classic fashion with Canarian potatoes and a *mojo* sauce.

🗺 169 E4 ✉ Calle La Garita 46
☎ 928 835 484 🕐 Fri–Wed noon–8

YAIZA

La Era €€€
The island's archetypal and most famous restaurant, La Era, was built as a farmhouse in the 17th century, restored by César Manrique and opened in 1970. It is set in a courtyard with a series of small rustic cosy dining rooms. It is not as cheap as it used to be but is still a must for traditional Canarian cooking (mainland Spanish specialities also available). Booking highly recommended.

🗺 168 B2 ✉ Calle El Barranco
☎ 928 830 016; www.laera.com
🕐 Tue–Sun 1–11

LA GERIA

Bodega El Chupadero €€
This little gem, deep in the heart of wine country, is only slightly off the beaten track but feels like a real discovery. It's a comfy tapas and snacks bar with bright soft cushions, modern art on the walls, ambient music, friendly staff and delicious slightly unusual food. Try the fresh tomato soup, the home-smoked salmon and crêpes. Highly recommended.

🗺 168 C2
✉ La Geria (for directions ➤ 120)
☎ 928 173 115; www.elchupadero.com
🕐 Tue–Sun noon–9

MOZAGA

Casa Museo del Campesino Restaurante €€–€€€
Beneath the César Manrique-designed landmark is a small rustic-style bodega (also Manrique-designed) which serves top-quality Canarian *picoteo* (snacks). A full menu devoted entirely to Canarian specialities can also be enjoyed here or in the large elegant circular restaurant below.

🗺 169 D2 ✉ San Bartolomé
☎ 928 520 136 🕐 Daily noon–4

HARÍA

El Cortijo €€€
This 200-year-old farmhouse has been beautifully restored. Sit inside the dark cosy rooms or on the large sunny terrace. Suckling pig, roast lamb, rabbit with rosemary and grilled meats are the specials.

🗺 169 E4
✉ El Palmeral
☎ 928 835 686 🕐 Daily noon–9

Lanzarote

Where to... Shop

PUERTO DEL CARMEN

The **Biosfera Plaza**, a ten-minute walk uphill from the port, is the best shopping centre in town and is open every day except Sunday until 11pm. Spread over four floors, it is home to international fashion outlets, souvenir shops and restaurants. You will find original lava jewellery in the Artesanía Volcánica (Planta 2), organic products in the Herbolario Eco-Spirit (Planta 1) and souvenirs from all over the world in Natura (Planta 1).

Artesanía Canaria sells handcrafted products from Lanzarote, **Arteberita** unusual art objects inspired by the island.

Next to the Plaza, in **Olalá,** you can find original souvenirs and jewellery.

La Tienda de las Cometas (Masdache, Carretera El Centro 1) stocks eye-catching kites in every size and colour imaginable – a fun thing to have on windy days on Fuerteventura.

ARRECIFE

The pedestrianised centre includes a wide range of shops that appeal to both islanders and visitors. The main street is Calle León y Castillo and you will find most of the main shops on or just off here. There are plenty of local stylish clothes and accessories shops too, such as Jack Jones or Tomás Panasco. At the far end of León y Castillo the **Atlantída** mall includes a Hiper-Dino department store.

Arrecife is at its most attractive on a Wednesday when there is a **crafts market** on the promenade.

TEGUISE

Teguise, the island's original capital, is famous for its Sunday market (▶118). However, at any time of the week it features the most stylish shops on the island, many of which are housed in beautifully converted centuries-old colonial houses.

There are no international brand-name shops, just individual enterprises. For island gifts look in at the **Tienda Artesanía** Lanzaroteña, Calzados y Mojos or Artesanía Guapa, all on the Plaza de la Constitución (main square next to the church).

On the adjacent Plaza Clavijo y Fajardo look into **Galleria La Villa** for exotic clothes. There is also a bookshop **(Leo).** In the next square, Plaza 18 de Julio, a shop has set up in the old hospital, offering locally made carpets and rugs.

It is worth popping into the **Emporium** (Calle Notas 15, www.emporium.es) just to admire its original setting. The former cinema now showcases Oriental furniture. Home accessories, jewellery, porcelain and decorative fabrics, most of which are imports from China and Tibet. A good address in the holiday resort Costa Teguise is **Pueblo Marinero,** another creation of the artist César Manrique. There you can, for instance, purchase pretty ceramics in La Tierra or a mischievous *El Dieblo* (the little mascot-cum-logo of the Timanfaya National Park), also designed by Manrique. Avoid Mondays and Saturdays when several shops are closed.

HARÍA

Haría, one of the island's prettiest villages (▶121), has a clutch of craft shops and if you are passing on a Saturday its **craft market**, held in the leafy main square, attracts the cream of the island's craftsfolk.

Insider Tip

Gran Canaria

Finding Your Feet	128
Getting Your Bearings	130
Don't Miss	132
At Your Leisure	134
Where to...	135

☼ Little Treats

Art temple
Just a few steps from the Casa de Colón (➤ 132), the **CAAM** exhibits modern art.

The islands' most beautiful town beach
After a visit to the Museo Canario (➤ 133), you can wander along the promenade of the **Playa de las Canteras**.

At the flea market
Every Sunday in **Rasto** (➤ 136), the vendors ply their colourful wares in the Parque de Santa Catalina.

Gran Canaria

Finding Your Feet

Flights from Fuerteventura

Inter-island flights are operated by Binter Canarias. There is a 30-minute check-in time and the flight time is 40 minutes. The journey from the airport to Las Palmas takes around 30 minutes, so you can catch the 8am flight from Fuerteventura and be in Las Palmas before 10am. A one-way fare costs – depending on the day and the date of the booking – around €52–€90. To book flights go to any travel agent, call 0034 902 391 392 or see www.bintercanarias.com

The first plane departs daily at 8am, and subsequent flights leave at regular intervals throughout the day. The last flights back from Gran Canaria are at 9:30pm (daily). This schedule is subject to change so check the timetable on the website. By catching the first and last flights you can spend at least ten hours in Las Palmas.

You must reserve your seats as far ahead as possible as the planes are small and the early flights will be in demand by business people.

Arriving at Gando Airport

The Aeropuerto de Gando is 22km (14mi) south of Las Palmas. The quickest but most expensive option is to take a taxi from outside the airport building. The journey time is around 20 minutes.

There is also a frequent reliable and inexpensive **bus service** to the capital. Bus 60 leaves from outside the airport terminal every 30 minutes from 6:30am to 9pm and then hourly until 2am. The journey takes around 30 minutes and arrives at the central bus station beside Parque de San Telmo in the heart of the city.

Tourist information offices

- The main office (tel: 928 219 600; www.grancanaria.com; open Mon–Fri 8–3) is at Calle León y Castillo 17, near the bus station.
- There is also an office at the airport at Arrivals Hall Gate A. They can help with overnight accommodation.
- There are information kiosks in Plaza de Hurtado Mendoza (open Mon–Fri 10–7:30, Sat 10–3); Avenida José Mesa y López (open Mon–Fri 10–3:30); Paseo de las Canteras (open Mon–Fri 10–7:30, Sat 10–3); and Parque de San Telmo (open Mon–Fri 10–7:30, Sat 10–3).
- If you want to check out what is going on in Las Palmas before you get there, see the official website above or www.lpavisit.com/en. These will also give you details of the city's famous Carnival celebrations.

Getting around

City buses
If you are only here for the day the most useful bus is No. 1 which runs between the old town (Parque de San Telmo) and the port (Parque de Santa Catalina).

The **Guagua Turística** (Tourist Bus) is a hop-on/hop-off tour bus that makes a two-hour circuit of the city beginning and ending in Parque de Santa Catalina (www.guaguas.com/turistica.htm). Tickets cost €14 and are valid for the day. The bus leaves Parque de Santa Catalina every half-hour from 9:30am–5:45pm. You can also pick up the bus from outside the central bus station at Parque de San Telmo.

Taxis
These operate as on Fuerteventura (▶ 37) and fares are very similar. For local journeys all fares are metered.

When to come
Avoid Monday when several attractions are closed and Sunday when the market and many shops are closed. If you want to see the excellent **folk dancing** at the Pueblo Canario (pictured on ▶ 127 and above) come on Thursday.

Carnival (February) can be a great time to visit Las Palmas as the celebrations here are massive compared with those on Fuerteventura. Plan your overnight stay for one of the days on which there is a procession as the actual fiesta itself will only just be warming up when it is time for you to fly back!

Flights, sailings and accommodation are at a real premium during *Carnaval* so you will need to book well ahead.

Timing it right
Many shops close for lunch between 1:30pm and 4:30pm though department stores and malls remain open throughout the day.

Gran Canaria

Getting Your Bearings

Cosmopolitan, buzzing with locals going about their daily business, teeming with shops, restaurants and a vibrant cultural life, Las Palmas is a real contrast to the wild landscapes of Fuerteventura. Whether you arrive by bus or by boat, the *Guagua Turística* (Tourist Bus) is perfectly placed to whisk you round the sights and shops of this exciting city.

Las Palmas stretches out like a long thin lizard along the island's north-eastern tip. The shape of the city has the effect of making it seem larger than it is. In fact, from Parque de Santa Catalina to Parque de San Telmo – the two reference points that will be of most use to day trippers – is around 3.5km (2mi).

The oldest part of town is the Vegueta District, around 800m south of Parque de San Telmo, with cobbled streets, shady squares and colonial-style architecture. It was founded by the island conqueror Juan Rejón in 1478 on a *vegueta* (meadow). Between Vegueta and Parque de San Telmo is Triana, an attractive mix of buildings spanning the 16th to 20th centuries. Here you will find lively shopping streets and open-air bars.

The area between Parque de San Telmo and Parque de Santa Catalina is residential, with the Pueblo Canario being the only point of visitor interest. Santa Catalina is the hub of the modern city and Playa de las Canteras, one of the finest city beaches in the world, is just a short walk away. Beyond the port, Puerto de la Luz, which is Spain's largest, the volcanic peaks of La Isleta provide a scenic backdrop.

Take in the colonial architecture in Plaza de Santa María and Triana

Getting Your Bearings

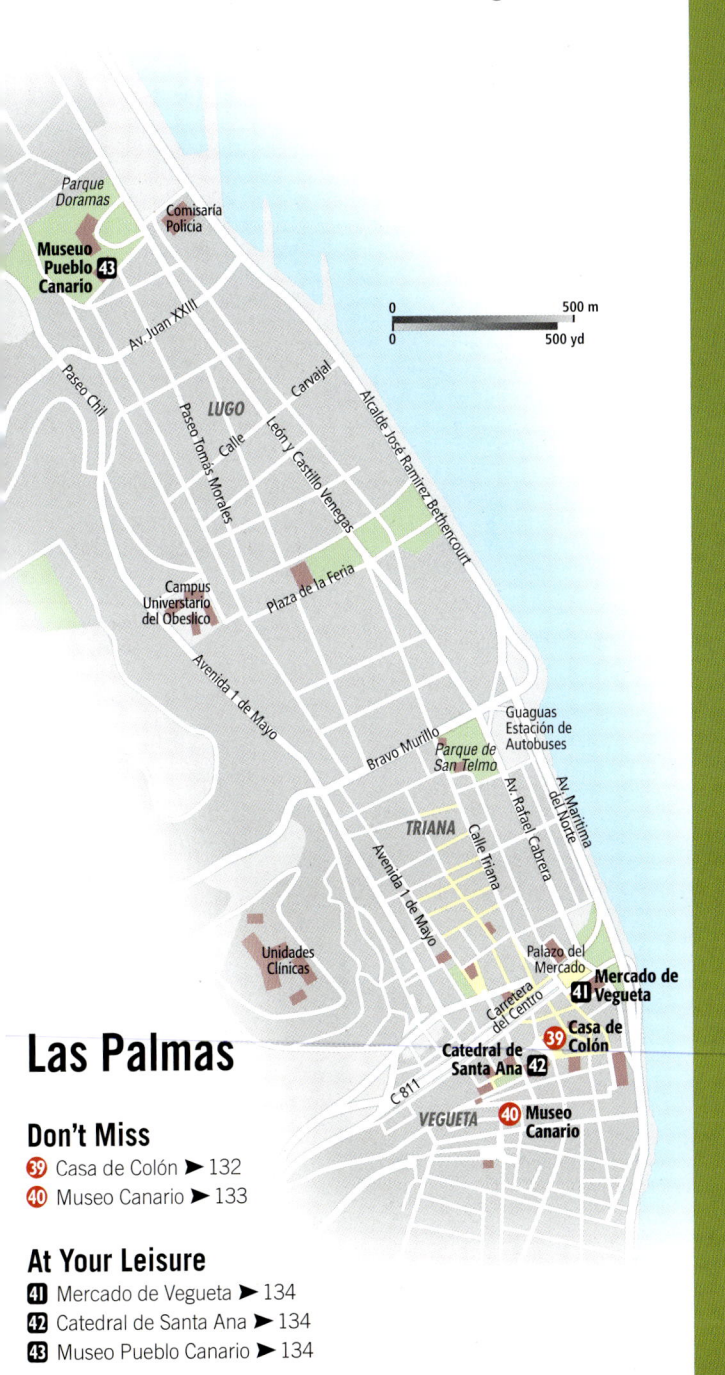

Las Palmas

Don't Miss
- ㊴ Casa de Colón ➤ 132
- ㊵ Museo Canario ➤ 133

At Your Leisure
- ㊶ Mercado de Vegueta ➤ 134
- ㊷ Catedral de Santa Ana ➤ 134
- ㊸ Museo Pueblo Canario ➤ 134

Gran Canaria

39 Casa de Colón

There is no proof that Christopher Columbus (Cristobal Colón in Spanish) ever stayed at this beautiful old house, but it is widely agreed that he did call at Las Palmas on the voyage that led to the "discovery" of the New World in 1492, and it is almost certain that he would have been offered accommodation here.

The Casa de Colón was originally the military governor's residence, one of the first buildings to be completed in Las Palmas following the Spanish conquest of 1478. It is a magnificent example of traditional Canarian colonial architecture, with carved stone portals, dark wooden balconies and richly ornamented facades. Today it is a museum dedicated to the explorer and his famous voyages.

If time is tight, concentrate on the ground-floor rooms as they offer the most interesting exhibits. Among the charts, navigational instruments and model boats, you will find a reconstruction of Columbus's cabin on board the *Santa María*; the log book of his first voyage to the New World; the seals of the Treaty of Tordesillas (1494), which carved the Atlantic into Spanish and Portuguese spheres of influence; and the map of the known world in 1500 by a cartographer who accompanied Columbus. The only thing missing is any personal possessions of Columbus himself.

The crypt is devoted to objects from the pre-Columbian period (ie, before 1492) and shows the richness of the native American cultures.

Immediately next door is the **CAAM** which has an impressive collection of modern art.

The splendid stone portal of the Casa de Colón

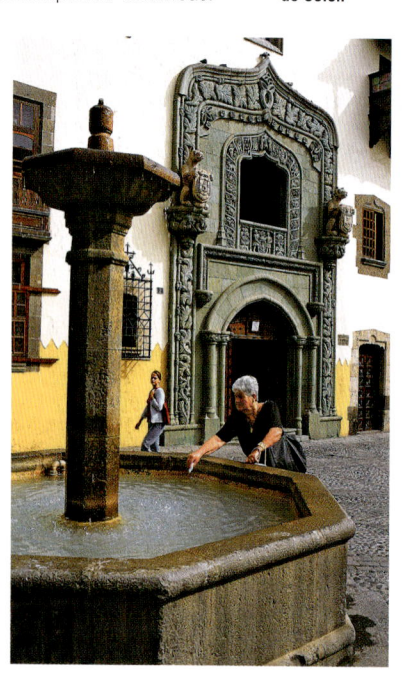

✚ 171 E1

Casa de Colón
✉ Calle Colón 1 ☎ 928 312 373;
www.casadecolon.com
🕐 Mon–Sat 10–6, Sun 10–3 💶 €4

CAAM (Centro Atlántico de Arte Moderno)
✉ Calle de los Balcones 9
☎ 928 31 18 00, www.caam.net
🕐 Tue–Sat 10–8, Sun 10–2 💶 €5

⓴ Museo Canario

This excellent museum is home to the archipelago's most comprehensive collection on the culture and lifestyle of the aboriginal Canarians known as the Guanches. You can see everything in around an hour.

Reconstructed wall paintings in the Cueva Pintada

The first three rooms are devoted to Guanche dwellings, agriculture and economy. If you are in a hurry, move swiftly through these to room four, the magic and religion gallery which contain original Guanche fertility idols, unmissable on account of their exaggerated genitalia (you will doubtless have seen some of these in the shops in Fuerteventura in reproduction form). The best known is the Idol of Tara (➤ 15), possibly symbolising the earth goddess. **Insider Tip**

Here also is a reproduction of the most famous Guanche dwelling yet discovered, the **Cueva Pintada** (Painted Cave) at Galdár on Gran Canaria plus a large collection of original *pintaderas* (wooden identity stamps), which again you will probably have seen on sale in reproduction form.

The most compelling sections of the museum are rooms six to nine, which deal with death and mummification. Some of the mummies are over 1.8m (6ft) high, showing that the Guanches were a tall race. There are also many skulls that have been trepanned, a surgical operation in which holes or incisions were made in the skull of a living person. It is not known whether this was done for medical or religious reasons.

The captions are all in Spanish, but the museum sells a guidebook with English and German translations.

✚ 171 E1
✉ Calle Dr Verneau 2
☎ 928 336 800; www.elmuseocanario.com
🕐 Mon–Fri 10–8, Sat–Sun 10–2 💷 €4

Gran Canaria

At Your Leisure

41 Mercado de Vegueta
The oldest, most colourful and most comprehensive market in the city (established 1854), this is where the locals come to buy a cornucopian range of fish, fruit, vegetables and cheese. Around the market are tapas bars and churrerías where people come to buy their *churros* (extruded dough fritters), which they dunk into cups of thick hot chocolate. *Insider Tip*
🕀 171 E1 ✉ Plaza del Mercado/Calle Mendizábal 🕒 Mon–Thu 6–2, Fri–Sat 6–3

42 Catedral de Santa Ana
The largest church in the Canary Islands dominates the Vegueta skyline. Begun in 1497 it took over 400 years to complete and so is a curious mix of Gothic, Renaissance, baroque and neo-Classical styles.

In its courtyard, replete with orange trees, is a beautiful cloister built in the late 16th century. A staircase leads to the chapter house, which has a handmade ceramic tile floor unique in the archipelago.

The cathedral interior is full of light and space and grand bishops' tombs. You need a separate ticket to ascend the tower in the lift.
🕀 171 E1 ✉ Plaza de Santa Ana (entrance on Calle Espirito Santo)
☎ 928 313 600
🕒 Outside of service times (daily 8–10), when entry to the cathedral is free, buy a ticket at the Museo Diocesano next door
🕒 Mon–Fri 10–4, Sat 10–1 💶 €3

44 Museo Pueblo Canario
This charming "village" of traditional Canarian buildings may seem like a tourist gimmick but it was designed as a serious attempt to preserve Canarian culture from the threat of mass tourism. The folk dancing is excellent but takes place only on Sundays at 11:30am. There are also shops, a café, a restaurant and the Museo Néstor, dedicated to the *moderniste* artist Nestor Fernandez de la Torre who created the village with his brother Miguel in the 1930s.
🕀 170 B5 ✉ Parque Doramas
☎ 928 242 985, Museum: 928 245 135; www.museonestor.com
🕒 Tue–Sat 10–8, Sun 10:30–2:30 (Museum Tue–Fri 10–8, Sun 10:30–2:30)
💶 Free; Museo Nestor: €2

PARK LIFE

Parque de San Telmo is the prettiest of the city parks and features a bandstand and a much-photographed *moderniste* (Spanish art nouveau) café inside a pavilion decorated with ceramic tiles. Parque de Santa Catalina is the throbbing hub of the city with cafés, newsstands, shops and the Museo Elder science museum. Tourists mingle with sailors, shoeshine boys, hustlers and African traders while old men play dominoes and chess beneath the palm trees.

Where to...
Eat and Drink

Prices
Expect to pay for a three-course meal for one, excluding drinks and service
€ under €15   €€ €15–€25   €€€ over €25

Most restaurants open throughout the year, though some take an annual holiday in August.

Café Santa Catalina €
This pleasant open-air café with a shady terrace beneath the palms is where the old locals gather to play chess and dominoes. The lunch menu is mostly standard fare such as pizzas and pastas but at any time it is an ideal place for an ice cream or a coffee and pastry.
off 170 B5 Parque Santa Catalina
Daily 10am–1am

Casa Carmelo €€–€€€
Renowned for the high quality of its grilled meats (particularly steak) and fish, and its special sauce, this traditional restaurant is popular with foreign visitors who also come to enjoy the great views across the beach.
off 179 B5 Paseo de las Canteras, 2
928 469 056; www.restaurantegrillcasacarmelo.com
Daily 1:30–4:30, 7:30–11:30

Casa Montesdeoca €€€
Close to the Casa Colón, this is the city's most elegant restaurant, situated in a 16th-century town house. You can just have a drink here but booking a table on the patio beneath the palms is something special. The service is very formal and the cooking is first class, featuring Canarian and Spanish dishes with the emphasis on fish.
171 E1 Calle Montesdeoca 10
928 333 466 Mon–Sat 1–4, 8–11:30

Don Quixote €€
Unwind from a shopping trip at this do-it-yourself restaurant where the speciality is *carne a la piedra* (steak, chicken or pork, cooked at the table on a hot stone). It comes with French fries, a big bowl of salad and a selection of relishes.
off 170 B5
Calle Diderot 3 679 159 080;
www.restaurantedonquixote.com
Thu–Mon 1–4, 8–midnight

La Marina €€–€€€
It is worth visiting La Marina just to enjoy the panorama from the terrace at the north end of the Playa de las Canteras. You have a wonderful view of the entire 3km (1.8mi) long sandy beach and the skyline of the Santa Catalina district. The restaurant's good fish dishes naturally means it is always busy at lunchtime; you pay for most of the fish by weight. There is also a delicious paella.
off 170 B5
Paseo de las Canteras 1
928 468 802;
www.restaurantelamarinera.info
Daily noon–midnight

Hotel Madrid €€
Enjoy an early evening or lunchtime drink and tapas outside this historic hotel set on one of the nicest squares in the city. The bar also serves reasonably priced set meals.
171 E1 Plaza de Cairasco 4
928 360 664 Daily 10am–1am

Gran Canaria

Where to... Shop

Most shops are open Monday to Saturday 10am to 8pm, although some close for lunch between 1:30pm and 4:30pm; the department stores open from 10am to 10pm.

Avenida Mesa y López
A five-minute walk south of Parque Santa Catalina, this is the main shopping street with two branches of Spain's most famous department store, **El Corte Inglés**, opposite each other. The main store has four floors of fashions and the Club del Gourmet features Canarian and Spanish food and wines. The top-floor café is a good place for a break. The second shop specialises in books, music, electronic goods, household items and souvenirs.

The rest of the Avenida is devoted to fashion and designer boutiques with famous international and top Spanish names.

Triana
Head for Calle Mayor La Triana in the heart of the old city. Formerly the main shopping street, it features some beautiful architecture with many shops retaining their *moderniste* (Spanish art nouveau) shop fronts. There are a few big names here but it is the quirky arty, crafty shops in the side streets which give this area its appeal. Look out for **Ezquerra** (Calle Travieso) for hats, *mantillas* (shawls) and Canarian desert boots.

Fedac (Calle Domingo J Navarro), a government-sponsored craft shop which sells a wide range of goods at very reasonable prices; **Casa Ricardo** (corner Calle Mayor and Calle Losero), the sweetshop of your childhood dreams; Calle Peregrina also contains several antiques shops. On Calle Triana 42 is a branch of **Natura Selection** offering fair-trade goods and crafts from around the world.

The best time to visit this area is from 6pm onwards during the early evening *paseo* (promenade) when locals and tourists take to the streets and buskers come out to entertain.

Parque de Santa Catalina
The area around the park is something of an Oriental bazaar with numerous Asian-run shops selling cheap cameras, watches, cigars, clothes and electronic goods.

The main streets are Calle de Tomás Miller, Calle Luis Morote and Calle Alfredo L Jones. Haggling is the norm so be prepared. Prices are not necessarily any keener than on Fuerteventura but there is a much larger range of stock here.

Markets
For food of all kinds visit the **Mercado de Vegueta** (▶ 134). If you are here on a Sunday morning, visit the lively **Rastro** (flea market) at Parque de Santa Catalina, which attracts many African traders with their colourful merchandise. The **Mercado de las Flores** on the Plaza de Santo Domingo (just south of the Museo Canario) sells arts, crafts and, as you would expect, flowers.

Malls
The biggest mall near the centre of town is **Las Arenas**, at the west end of Playa de Las Canteras and close to one of the stops on the Guagua Turistica bus route. A further large consumer temple is **El Muelle** at the harbour.

Pueblo Canario
This complex of traditionally built island houses provides very pleasant relaxed surroundings in which to buy top-quality souvenirs, craft items, ceramics, books and Gran Canarian folk music (▶ 134).

> Insider Tip

Walks & Tours

1 Isla de Lobos	138
2 Sendero de Bayuyo	142
3 Highlights in North and Central Fuerteventura	145
4 Coast-to-Coast	150

Walks & Tours

1 ISLA DE LOBOS
Walk

DISTANCE 10km (6mi)
TIME 2hrs 30mins–3hrs
START/END POINT El Muelle (the harbour) ✚ 163 F5

You will feel like a desert island explorer here. Lobos is a microcosm of "the mainland" with mini-volcanoes, small lagoons, a superb little beach, a tiny ramshackle fishing village, a picturesque lighthouse and mountaintop views that equal any on Fuerteventura. Choose a clear day to enjoy it. You need a modicum of fitness to climb the mountain; while boots are not necessary, sturdy trainers are a minimum requirement. See ➤ 48 for more on the island.

Getting to the starting point
There are three boats that run daily to the island from Corralejo. If you want to eat on the island as well as fit in sunbathing, choose the service that gives you the most time. (For more details ➤ 48.) If it is very windy, it is better to cancel the excursion to the island.

❶–❷
On disembarking at **El Muelle**, turn right, following the signpost towards "El Puertito 7 mins" and "Las Lagunitas 18 mins". **El Puertito**

As usual, there is not much going on in the small fishing village of El Puertito

Isla de Lobos

("the little port") is possibly the most tumbledown fishing village you will ever see, little more than a motley collection of a dozen or so wooden and stone shacks that have seen better days. Pass through (it doesn't take long!) and fork right to head to the sea. The path is well marked, and anyway the island is too small to get lost. At the edge of a small promontory you look out across to Lanzarote. To your right is **Las Lagunitas** ("the little lagoons"), a sandy salt marsh where migratory birds come to feed and rest.

2–3

As you reach the end of the salt flats the path turns right towards the sea but this is no more than a short detour. Ignore it and keep going straight ahead following the trail up a slight incline to the left where it leads to what appears to

139

Walks & Tours

> **TAKING A BREAK**
> If you intend to eat at the island restaurant you MUST make a reservation as soon as you land. Beware, however, that if you are going to take a leisurely walk around the island you may not get back until around 2pm (later if you spend a long time on the beach!). This should still give you just enough time to eat but check what time they stop serving. There is no menu as such, but the choice is generally paella or fresh fish.
>
> Bring a sunshade, hat and plenty of water. The restaurant sells water and will make you a basic tuna *bocadillo* (baguette) but unless you have booked for lunch that's the top and bottom of the refreshment options. They do have ice creams but these are reserved for restaurant customers!

be a small white tin shelter. In fact, as you get closer this turns out to be the underneath of an information board on the flora and fauna of Las Lagunitas. Look across the island and you can see right back to the dunes of Corralejo. A broad sandy path leads from here to the **Faro de Lobos** (lighthouse) and should take you another 25 to 30 minutes.

Just before you reach the Faro at Punta Martiño, the northernmost part of the island, you pass by a number of small brown protuber-

View of the Isla de Lobos

ances, typically around 3–8m (10–26ft) high. These are *hornitos* (literally "little ovens"), mini-volcanoes, formed not in the usual way, by magma pushing up the earth, but by steam-driven explosions (known technically as phreatic eruptions) that occur when water beneath the ground is heated by magma, lava, hot rocks or new volcanic activity. These were created some 8,000 years ago and are best appreciated from the lighthouse which sits on a large raised concrete base. From here there are also tremendous views

Isla de Lobos

Constant companions on the seashore: the seagulls are true flying artists

across to Lanzarote. The resort of Playa Blanca and its Papagayo beaches are ahead of you and looming above them are the Montañas del Fuego (➤ 114–115), while to the right the metropolis of blurred white blocks is Puerto del Carmen. Rejoin the path which turns almost back on itself at this point.

3–4

Continue on the broad sandy path for around 15 minutes. The **Montaña de la Caldera** looms large to your right but avoid the temptation to take the first turn off to the right, which in fact leads to Caleta del Palo. Take the next path right – "Montaña de la Caldera 30 mins". This refers to the time it takes to reach the 127m-high (416ft) summit. This is quite a steep climb so take it easy, particularly as the steps finish about three-quarters of the way up and the last part is a bit of a scramble. It's well worth the effort, however. The 360-degree views covering the three islands of Fuerteventura, Lanzarote and Lobos itself are exhilarating.

The excursion boats and catamarans anchored off the white-sand bay to your left are a picture, while way down below, on the other side of the ridge, is the almost perfect semicircular stone beach of **Caleta del Palo**, right inside the mountain crater. You can quite safely walk a long way right along the ridge looking down onto Corralejo, though do take care if it's a windy day.

4–5

Descend the mountain and return to the main track. Turn right and it's a five-minute walk to the lovely little white sand crescent of **Playa de la Caleta**. This is an ideal spot for family bathing, with very calm waters and a gently sloping sandy bottom. From here it's a three-minute stroll back to the harbour.

> **BIRD ISLAND**
> The Isla de Lobos is rarely crowded. When you disembark, just wait a bit until everyone else has walked on ahead – then you can have the island all to yourself – or at least feel like you have it all to yourself. In actual fact, you are surrounded by living things: about 140 different species of plant grow here and the entire island is a bird sanctuary. Look out for a *Pardela Cenicienta* (Cory's Shearwater); this large seabird has a slow and elegant style of flight.

Walks & Tours

2 SENDERO DE BAYUYO
Walk

> **DISTANCE** 5km/3mi (9km/5mi if you continue on to Corralejo)
> **TIME** 2hrs–2hrs 30mins
> **START/END POINT** Just north of Lajares ✚ 163 D4

The Sendero de Bayuyo was the first of what is now a well-developed network of marked hiking trails. It takes you past dramatic volcanic formations, shows the harsh conditions of goat herding and offers wonderful views to the north of the island and beyond.

To find the start of the walk, take the FV109 to **Lajares** from **Corralejo**. Just before Lajares, opposite the Witchcraft Surf Shop (on the left), look to your right and you will see a curious purple-brown volcano with two depressions that resemble large eyes – this is where you are heading! To get there continue for 0.5km to the football ground and turn right just in front of it. Continue for 1km (0.6mi) past a sign to the Zoo Safari Calderon Hondo (now closed down) and park past the last house on the right-hand side of the road. A path cobbled with rough black volcanic stones marks the way.

1–2

Follow the black brick road. The pock-marked volcano that you saw from the main road, the **Montaña Colorada** (Coloured Mountain), which rises

142

Sendero de Bayuyo

to 240m (790ft), should always be to your left. Look back and you can see the little white houses of Lajares. The path disappears briefly but veer to the right and you will soon pick it up again. Look out over the black *malpaís* (rough volcanic debris) to your right. *Malpaís* translates as "bad steps", which you will appreciate if you leave the path and try to traverse it (this is not recommended!). It was formed some 8,000 years ago and is speckled grey-green with lichen, a fungi which is a very good indicator of air pollution. As long as the air is pure the lichen will thrive. After about 20 minutes of walking, the **Montaña Colorada** dips in a saddle. You will notice a number of holes in the volcano; they are the result of quarrying for pumice, a popular raw material in road construction. You will come to a small hill from the top of which you can see the snow-white dunes of Corralejo (▶ 50).

2-3

After around 30 minutes you will pass through a low drystone wall. Due north on the horizon is Playa Blanca, Lanzarote and its mountains. After another five to ten minutes the path forks. Go left and ignore the two smaller paths turning off to the right. After three to four minutes of steep climbing you will reach a viewing platform at an altitude of 230m (755ft). This not only offers a wonderful panorama but also lets you peer right down into the extinct, perfectly round crater of the volcano. Look to your left and you will see a spectacular "cowl" that shows how the

TAKING A BREAK
There is little shade available and on hot days you should thus remember to take plenty of water with you. There are several good places in Lajares for lunch (▶ 60).

Walks & Tours

TIME IT RIGHT
Although this landscape is harsh and barren for much of the year, in spring there is a surprising amount of foliage around. Try to time the walk so that you end as the sun is going down, when the volcanoes are tinged with purple and amber.

volcano collapsed. Down in the crater prickly pears are growing, while a family of goats often graze and laze right by the crater edge. You can skirt part of the crater lip but take care, and it is not recommended to try to walk right around it. The panorama in front of you stretches from the little white fishing village of Majanicho to the west (left) to the distant white blur of Puerto del Carmen on Lanzarote to the east. Peer closely and just outside Majanicho you can see the outline of a new housing development. In the middle distance to the east stands the **volcano of Bayuyo** at 271m (889ft).

3–4
Descend the path and take the second fork left to the goat **herders' building** that you could see from the top of Calderón Hondo.

Look inside this primitive shelter (it is a replica purpose-built for visitors) and you will see its thatch and mud roof construction set on volcanic drystone walls. The small conical construction nearby shows how a primitive oven was fashioned. A corral has also been made from the volcanic debris.

4–1
At this point you can either head back the way you came or extend the walk by exploring the volcanoes that you have seen from your viewpoint. Use Bayuyo as your guide point, follow the path and in an hour or so you will be standing below it. If you want to climb the summit it takes around 30 minutes and offers wonderful views down into Corralejo's "backyard". **Corralejo** itself is another hour or so walk away.

A view of the Montaña Colorada with its deep holes. In the afternoon, the reddish volcanic mountains are particularly colourful

Highlights in North and Central Fuerteventura

3 HIGHLIGHTS IN NORTH AND CENTRAL FUERTEVENTURA
Drive

DISTANCE 151km/94mi (with options for short cuts)
TIME Full day
START/END POINT Corralejo 163 E5

This full-day drive will show you the best of north and central Fuerteventura. The roads are fast and straight in the north, often slow and tortuous in the heart of the island, but well worth the effort with magnificent mountain scenery.

1-2

Begin in **Corralejo** (distances are taken from the roundabout by the football ground). After 1km (0.5mi) go right at the next roundabout and take the FV101 to La Oliva. To your right is the **Volcan de Bayuyo**, rising to 271m (889ft).

After 13km (8mi) you will pass through one of the island's best-kept villages, **Villaverde** (➤ 56). Two adjacent windmills form a backdrop and, as you are about to leave the village, note the **Hotel Rural Mahoh** (➤ 62), built in the vernacular style with immaculate gardens. Just before you reach the centre of **La Oliva** (➤ 53), notice the ruined Casa del Inglés to your right. A one-way system takes you round the right hand side of the

An isolated location: Ermita La Virgen de la Peña, not far from Vega de Río Palmas

village centre, but as you pass the **Centro de Arte Canario** (➤ 53) look straight ahead to the perfectly triangular cone of Montaña de Frontón, which provides a spectacular backdrop.

2-3

Continue through the centre of La Oliva on the FV10 towards Puerto del Rosario and after 5km (3mi) the sacred mountain of **Tindaya** (➤ 57) looms on your right. After another 2–3km (1–2mi)

TIME IT RIGHT
There are several museums and attractions on this route so if you want the option of visiting them it is best to **avoid Mondays and Saturdays** when most are closed. None of them are "must see", though the most interesting are the Ecomuseo de La Alcogida at Tefia and the Casa de Santa María at Betancuria.

145

Walks & Tours

look to your right and standing in front of the 399m-high (1,309ft) Montaña Quemada you will see what appears to be a tiny statue dwarfed by the mountain. It is in fact the 2.3m-high (7.5ft) monument to **Miguel de Unamuno** (➤ 76). Shortly after this, turn right, onto the FV207. The road swoops down into a mostly empty valley with just a few homesteads amid the fields. After 7km (4 mi) you come to the little village of Tefia. Just as you leave the village there is a much-photographed **molina** to the right (➤ 73) and after a few hundred metres on your left is the **Ecomuseo de La Alcogida** (➤ 74), usually with a pair of donkeys and a camel in a roadside field.

Half-day option

If the Ecomuseo de La Alcogida detains you and you want to turn this drive into a half-day tour, head back north from Tefia and turn right onto the FV10. Go through Tetir then, after around 15km (9mi), just before the coast and the outskirts of Puerto del Rosario, follow the FV3 ring road to the left towards Corralejo. Then simply hug the coastline all the way back (some 35km/22mi) to Corralejo.

Highlights in North and Central Fuerteventura

and Casa del Queso so there is no need to break your journey yet. After another 2km (1mi) turn right towards Betancuria and the road winds tightly upwards. Look high above you and you can see what seems to be a large chalet-style building with picture windows. It is the **Mirador de Morro Veloso**. Stop here and admire the wonderful view north. (If for any reason the mirador is not open, there is a place where you can pull off the road almost adjacent to it and enjoy the same view.)

4-5

The old capital of **Betancuria** is full of sightseeing interest and can easily occupy a half-day in its own right (➤ 70). Continue through Betancuria glancing down below to your right just after you pass through the centre to see the roofless ruin of the Convent of San Buenaventura. As you leave Betancuria behind, palm trees are much in evidence on this stretch of road together with metal wind pumps, some of them dating back to the 1930s. After 5km (3mi) you will pass the pretty little church of **Vega de Río Palmas**.

After another 1km (0.6mi) or so there is a pull-off point on the right from which you can look down onto the **Embalse de las Peñitas** (reservoir). If it is dry it looks like a large brown field, though unnaturally straight and flat. Beside it, nestled in to the gully and just visible, is the ancient little white chapel of **La Virgen de**

3-4

Continue for 6km (4mi) and turn right on the FV30 towards Betancuria. The road now starts to climb and the pretty little roadside hamlet of **Valle de Santa Inés**, with its Artesanía and Casa del Queso, is a "starter" for the "main course" of **Betancuria** (➤ 70). If you intend stopping in the old island capital (and it is highly recommended) it too has an Artesanía

---

TAKING A BREAK

If you made a late start and fancy a fish lunch after passing through Tefia, take the turning right onto the FV221 and drive 11km (7mi) to the pretty little port of Los Molinos (➤ 75) where there are two good seaside restaurants.

Walks & Tours

> **THE SHORT WAY BACK**
> Just north of La Ampuyenta you have the option of returning to Corralejo through Tefia. If you want to take this option, turn left on the FV30 towards Valle de Santa Inés, then right towards Tefia on the FV207.

la Peña, the island's patron saint. The road winds upwards again, passing through mountains that resemble melted chocolate, and reaches one of the highlights of this tour, the **Degollada de los Granadillos**. Pull off the road to enjoy the spectacular views east and west; a stylised whitewashed portal, marking the provincial boundary, stands in stark relief to the dark brown mountain scenery and gives this pass even greater drama.

Continue onto Pajara staying on the FV30 towards Gran Tarajal.

5-6

After the barren mountains of the Betancuria province, pretty **Pájara** (➤ 77) is an oasis of colour. Park by the church and even if it is closed do have a look at its portal. Continue ahead with the church to your left. After 9km (6mi) turn left at the town of Tuineje onto the FV20 towards Antigua and Puerto del Rosario.

Aloe vera is cultivated in some of the fields around the town. If the

> **DETOUR**
> Somewhat confusingly, 1km (0.5mi) or so after the church of Vega de Río Palmas, another sign leads off right also to Vega de Río Palmas. This pleasant side road winds through palm groves and runs more or less parallel to the main road. It finishes in a dead end after around 3km (2mi) overlooking the **Embalse de las Peñitas** (reservoir) (➤ 147).

parish church is open, call in to see the altarpiece, which depicts the Battle of Tamasite in 1740, when the locals repelled a raid by British privateers.

Tiscamanita lies 4km (2.5mi) north and its **Centro de Interpretación de los Molinos** (➤ 78) is just north of the centre. From here, the road to Antigua is straight and fast but enjoy the scenery to your left with mountains running along the spine of the island. Largest of all is the Gran Montaña, which at 708m (2,322ft) is one of the island's highest peaks.

6-7

Stop off in the centre of the appealing old town of **Antigua** (➤ 73), have a look at the church and then head north for 1–2km (0.6–1mi) to reach the **Molino de Antigua** (➤ 73) a 200-year-old windmill. With its garden, plaza and cafeteria (➤ 79) it's a good place for a break. After another 2–3km (1–2mi) you will come to the small town of La Ampuyenta, home to the **Casa-Museo Dr Mena**, which is a fine example of a large, comfortable, upper-class country house dating from the 19th century (currently closed). The village's 17th-century **Ermita de San Pedro de Alcántara** chapel is also worth a look.

7-8

Continue on the FV20 towards Puerto del Rosario to **Casillas del Angel** where the Iglesia de Santa Ana contains an 18th-century carving of St Anne. After 5km (3mi) turn left at Llano Pelado onto the FV225. Fork off left after 2–3km (1–2mi) and head towards Tetir. This pretty little village is worth a coffee stop before continuing on the FV10 through La Oliva and back north to Corralejo.

The area around Tuineje is relatively fertile and there is a lot of agriculture here

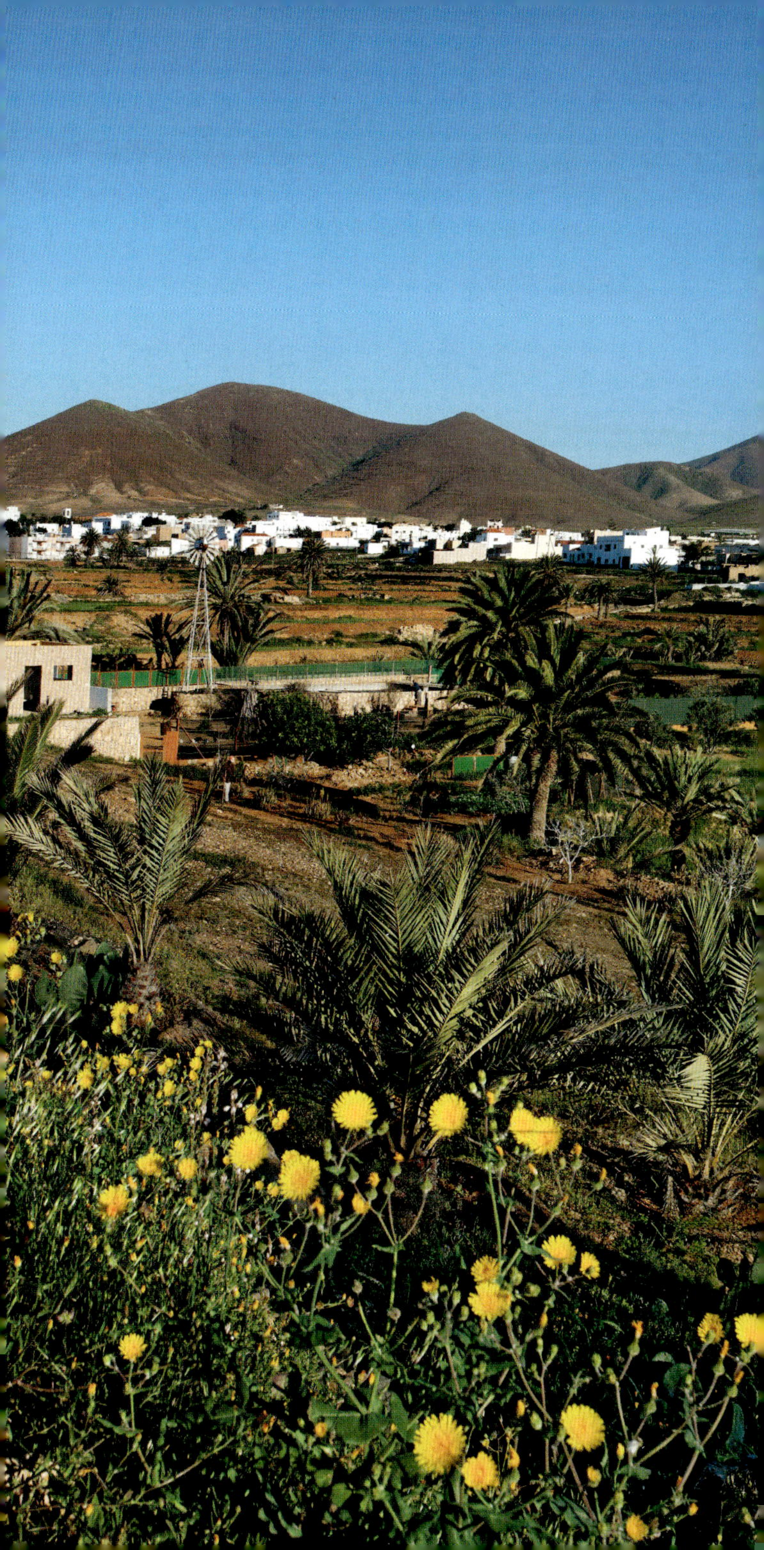

Walks & Tours

4 COAST-TO-COAST
Walk

DISTANCE 10km (6mi)
TIME Around 3hrs
START/END POINT Centro Commercial El Palmeral, Costa Calma ✚ 167 E3

This easy walk crosses La Pared isthmus at its narrowest point. It's a mere 3km (2mi) stroll from the manicured hotel grounds and shopping centres of Costa Calma to the wild windswept wave-beaten Barlovento coastline. This is a golden opportunity to see the beaches of the west without the need for a 4WD vehicle.

SWIMMING
Do take along your swimming kit or simply bare all as many people do on these beaches. There are a few small protected lagoon areas along this stretch where you may (just) be able to immerse yourself completely, but you MUST beware that it is highly dangerous to swim anywhere in open water on the west coast due to the treacherous currents and undertows.

1–2
The track on which this walk begins lies some 500m behind the **El Palmeral Shopping Centre**. You can walk to the beginning of the track by taking the road immediately to the right-hand side

Costa Calma is one of the tourist strongholds, but you can still find quiet spots

Coast-to-Coast

of the centre, next to the Hodge Podge (Calle Playa de la Jaqueta) clothing shop. This is a one-way system, so if you want to drive you will have to go around the petrol station to the left of the shopping centre, turn right, then take the second left into Calle Playa de la Jacquete. Park at the very end by the pylon where the road ends and the track begins. Almost immediately to your left as you begin the walk is the **Parque Eólico Cañada de la Barca** wind farm The 45 modern turbines make an important contribution to providing the island with sustainable energy.

2–3

Many parallel tracks cross the island at this point but simply follow your nose as they all head due west. This is a popular walk so you will rarely be on your own. Away to your right (the north west) the hills and low mountains often sit broodily. It may be bright sunshine on the trail yet quite dark in the distance.

What you are walking on is a mix of ancient jable (dune field) of solidified sand, covered in saltpetre, and a more recent jable made up of dunes blown across the isthmus by the trade winds from the west coast. The sands

TAKING A BREAK
Don't do this walk if it is a windy day as you risk being sandblasted and half-blinded by dust and sand. Take plenty of water with you. The Fuerte Action Bar in the El Palmeral Shopping Centre is a good place for lunch or a snack at the end of your walk.

Walks & Tours

The *Chlamydotis undulata* is one of the rarest birds on the island

are held together by small scrubby plants chewed by goats.

3-4
You reach the west coast after about 40 minutes of walking, emerging at the cliffs of **Agua Tres Piedras**. Step down carefully to the beach and look at the weird eroded shapes that have been caused in the alternating layers of basalt and fossilized sand. It may not be apparent to the human eye, but at the base of this escarpment there are natural springs that provide a welcome watering hole for birds and livestock.

Continue along the narrow ledge close to the water's surface: the eroded shapes become more spectacular. A huge sand dune slopes right down to the beach. A little further north black lava outflows provide a lagoon area and rock pools for paddling. The power of the sea is demonstrated by the large waves which create a spectacular show by breaking off the rocks high into the air. You cannot swim here (➤ note on Swimming, page 151) and if you're exploring the rock pools beware that some of the crabs around here are quite large!

It takes around another five to ten minutes to walk along the coast to reach **Los Boquetes**, a spectacular little bay with bright red layers of rock. On the far side, walk out to the end of the point and enjoy great views up and down the coast. A wall of rock blocks progress much further up the coast so it's time to turn back.

4-1
From here you can either return the way you came, which is the easiest option, or negotiate your way over the dunes and return to Costa Calma by paths that run parallel to the one you came on. Break the journey back with a picnic at one of the beaches.

GROUND SQUIRRELS AND BUSTARDS

Ornithologists should keep an eye out for the endangered *Chlamydotis undulata* , a type of bustard endemic to the Canary Islands and North Africa (photo above). Sadly, due to the loss of its habitat, the breeding population in the whole archipelago is down to less than 400 pairs. One creature you are likely to see is the ground squirrel, scampering around the rocks by the seaside.

Practicalities

Before You Go 154
When You are There 156
Useful Words and Phrases 159

Practicalities

BEFORE YOU GO

WHAT YOU NEED

● Required
○ Suggested
▲ Not required

Some countries require a passport to remain valid for a minimum period (usually at least six months) beyond the date of entry – check beforehand.

	UK	USA	Canada	Australia	Ireland	Netherlands	Germany
Passport/National Identity Card	●	●	●	●	●	●	●
Visa (regulations can change – check before booking)	▲	▲	▲	▲	▲	▲	▲
Onward or Return Ticket	○	●	●	●	○	○	○
Health Inoculations (tetanus and polio)	▲	▲	▲	▲	▲	▲	▲
Health Documentation (➤ 158, Health)	●	▲	▲	▲	●	●	●
Travel Insurance	○	○	○	○	○	○	○
Driving Licence (national)	●	●	●	●	●	●	●
Car Insurance Certificate	●	●	●	●	●	●	●
Car Registration Document	●	●	●	●	●	●	●

WHEN TO GO

High season   Low season

JAN	FEB	MAR	APRIL	MAY	JUNE	JULY	AUG	SEP	OCT	NOV	DEC
22°C	23°C	26°C	22°C	25°C	26°C	26°C	28°C	26°C	26°C	24°C	23°C
72°F	73°F	79°F	72°F	77°F	79°F	79°F	82°F	79°F	79°F	75°F	73°F

☀ Sun   ⛅ Sun/Showers

The temperatures above are the **average daily maximum** for each month. Minimum temperatures rarely drop below 15°C (59°F); a year-round spring climate means that average temperatures range from 19°C (66°F) in winter to 26°C (79°F) in summer. The sea temperature varies from 19°C (66°F) in January to 24°C (75°F) in September. Most of the rain falls in the north while the Jandía isthmus in the south enjoys almost uninterrupted sunshine. The North-East trade wind influences the weather, and guarantees that there is always a fresh breeze, which is one of the main reasons why this location has become such a top destination for windsurfers and kitesurfers. **The high season** is from November to April and July and August, when many Spanish families are on holiday. The quietest months are May, June, September and October.

GETTING ADVANCE INFORMATION

Websites
- www.visitfuerteventura.es
- www.fuerteventuraturismo.com
- www.fuerteventura.com

Other sites worth a look are www.fuertenews.com, an English-language weekly magazine and their offshoot island guide, www.fuerteventura.com/grapevine

Practicalities

GETTING THERE

By air There are numerous charter flights throughout the year from London and other European cities. Most seats are sold by tour operators as part of a package holiday, but it is possible to buy a flight-only deal though travel agents on the internet. For independent travellers, the disadvantage of charter flights is that you are usually restricted to a period of either seven or 14 days.

The Spanish national airline, **Iberia**, operates regular scheduled flights to Fuerteventura, but these are expensive and unless you are already living in Spain they are not worth considering.

You can also fly to the neighbouring island of Lanzarote. From the Playa Blanca ferry harbour, boats leave every 20 minutes for Corralejo on Fuerteventura (➤ 36).

By sea The ferry company **Trasmediterránea** has a weekly car ferry service from Cádiz on the Spanish mainland to Tenerife and Gran Canaria. The journey from Cádiz to Las Palmas takes around 50 hours (www.trasmediterranea.es/en).

Inter-island travel

By air Binter Canarias (www.bintercanarias.com) offer daily flights from Fuerteventura to the other Canary Islands.

By sea Naviera Armas (tel: 902 456 500; www.naviera-armas.com) operate from Puerto del Rosario and Morro Jable to Las Palmas de Gran Canaria (www.navieraarmas.com). There is also a high-speed ferry (www.fredolsen.es) from Playa Blanca (Lanzarote) to Corralejo (Fuerteventura).

TIME

Unlike the rest of Spain, the Canary Islands observe Greenwich Mean Time (GMT). Summer time (GMT+1) operates from the last Sunday in March to the last Sunday in October

CURRENCY & FOREIGN EXCHANGE

Currency As in the rest of Spain, the Canary Islands have adopted the euro. Notes are in denominations of 5, 10, 20, 50, 100, 200, 500; coins come in 1, 2, 5, 10, 20 and 50 cents and 1 and 2 euros.

Credit cards Major credit cards are widely accepted in the resorts, but don't rely on these elsewhere.

Exchange Banks generally offer the best rates for changing foreign currency and travellers' cheques though money can be exchanged at travel agents, hotels and exchange bureaus. When changing travellers' cheques you will need to show your passport. You can also withdraw cash from **ATM (cashpoint) machines** using your credit or debit card and PIN. The rate of exchange is often better than what you will get elsewhere though your account holder will usually make a charge for this service.

TOURIST OFFICES OF SPAIN ➤ WWW.SPAIN.INFO

In the UK
2nd floor,
79 New Cavendish Street,
London W1W 6XB
☎ 020 7486 8077
www.tourspain.co.uk

In the US
666 Fifth Ave (35th Floor)
New York NY 10103
☎ 212/265-8822
www.okspain.org

Tourist Office of Spain
1221 Brickell Ave
Miami FL 33131
☎ 305/358-1992

Practicalities

WHEN YOU ARE THERE

NATIONAL HOLIDAYS

1 Jan	New Year's Day
6 Jan	Epiphany
19 Mar	St Joseph's Day
Mar/Apr	Good Friday, Easter Monday
1 May	Labour Day
30 May	Canary Islands' Day
May/June	Corpus Christi
25 July	St James
15 Aug	Assumption of the Virgin
12 Oct	Columbus Day
1 Nov	All Saints' Day
6 Dec	Constitution Day
8 Dec	Feast of the Immaculate Conception
25 Dec	Christmas Day

ELECTRICITY

The power supply is 220–225 volts. Sockets take standard continental-style plugs with two round pins.

Visitors from the UK require an adaptor (often available at the airport). Visitors from the USA will require a voltage transformer.

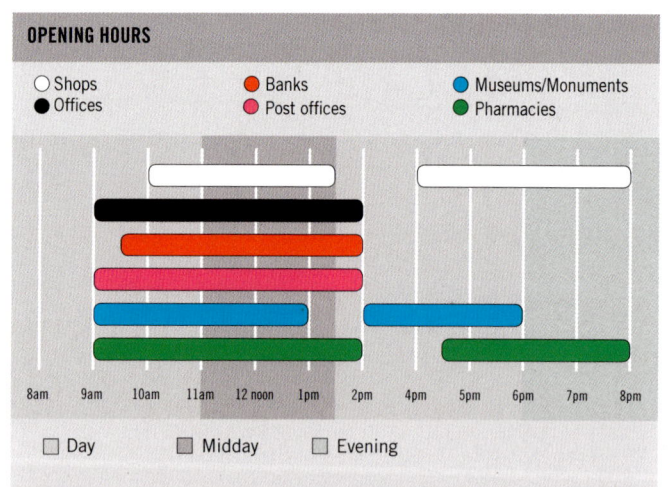

OPENING HOURS

- ○ Shops
- ● Offices
- ● Banks
- ● Post offices
- ● Museums/Monuments
- ● Pharmacies

☐ Day ☐ Midday ☐ Evening

Shops Many shops in the resorts stay open throughout the day. Most shops are closed on Sundays.
Banks Mainly open Mon–Fri, 9:30am–2pm, sometimes on Sat as well.
Post Offices Usual times are Mon–Fri 9am–2pm, Sat until 1pm.
Museums Most museums are open Tue–Fri, Sun 9:30am–5:30pm. Some close at midday for a couple of hours.

TIME DIFFERENCES

Fuerteventura	London (GMT)	Mainland Spain (CET)	New York (EST)	Sydney (AEST)
12 noon	12 noon	1pm	7am	10pm

Practicalities

STAYING IN TOUCH

Post Post boxes are yellow and often have a slot marked *extranjeros* for mail abroad. Stamps *(sellos)* are available from post offices, hotels, news kiosks, tobacconists and some postcard shops. A postcard to the UK or northern Europe will usually take about 7–12 days.

Telephones The cheapest way of making calls is to go to a *locutorio*. These can be found all over the island, in shopping centres or even as part of a local grocer's or souvenir shop. You are allocated a booth and then charged for the call afterwards. They are very cheap indeed and a 20-minute call to mainland Europe in the evening costs little more than a couple of euros.

There are public telephones on most street corners with instructions in several languages. Most take coins or phonecards (*tarjetas telefónicas*), which are available from several outlets, though in practice they are not always stocked.

International Dialling Codes
Dial 00 followed by:
UK:	44
Ireland:	353
USA/Canada:	1
Australia:	61

Mobile providers and services: Mobile phones automatically tune in to the partner network. Purchasing a local prepaid card can be less expensive. The Spanish word for mobile phone is *móvil*.

PERSONAL SAFETY

Crime is not a problem in Fuerteventura. Tourists rarely experience violence. Thieves do break into vehicles and steal personal items, however. Put all belongings out of sight in the boot of your car when you are parked. If you are in self-catering accommodation lock all windows and doors before going out.

In an emergency call the police on 112 from any phone.

Police assistance:
☎ 112 from any phone

TIPS/GRATUITIES

Tipping is not expected for all services.
As a general guide:
Restaurants: up to 10%
Tour guides, Porters and Chambermaids: €1
Cafés/bars, Taxis, Toilets, Hairdressers: Small change

POLICE (POLICÍA NACIONAL)	112
FIRE (BOMBEROS)	112
AMBULANCE (AMBULANCIA)	112

Practicalities

HEALTH

Insurance Citizens of the European Union and certain other countries receive free medical treatment in Spain with the relevant documentation, although private medical insurance is still advised and is essential for all other visitors.

Dental Services Dental treatment has to be paid for by all visitors but is usually covered by private medical insurance.

Weather Visitors from cooler countries are especially vulnerable to the effects of the sun. You should cover up with a high-factor sunblock and drink plenty of non-alcoholic fluids. Children need to be well protected, especially when playing near the sea, as water and sand reflect the sun's rays.

Drugs Prescription and non-prescription drugs and medicines are available from pharmacies, usually distinguished by a large green cross. Outside normal hours, a notice on the door of each pharmacy should give the address of the nearest duty pharmacist.

Safe Water Tap water is generally safe to drink, although it does not taste particularly good because it comes from desalination plants. Mineral water *(agua mineral)* is widely available and cheap, especially when bought at supermarkets in 5-litre (1.3-gallon) containers.

CONCESSIONS

Students There are few if any youth or student concessions. There are no youth hostels or campsites on the island although there is a basic campsite on Isla de Lobos.
Senior Citizens Fuerteventura is an excellent destination for older travellers, especially in winter when the climate is clement. Some hotels and apartments offer long-stay discounts, as does the airline Binter and the ferry line Fred Olsen.

TRAVELLING WITH A DISABILITY

All new buildings in Spain have to be equipped with wheelchair access, but many older hotels, apartment blocks and public buildings are still inaccessible. Some buses have doors that lower to ground level for wheelchair access. Before booking a holiday, you should discuss your particular needs with your tour operator or hotel.

CHILDREN

Hotels and restaurants are generally very child-friendly. However, facilities such as baby-changing rooms are rare. Special attractions for kids are marked out using the logo above.

RESTROOMS

There are public lavatories in shopping centres and at some larger beaches. Other useful standbys are museums and bars.

CUSTOMS

The import of wildlife souvenirs sourced from rare or endangered species may be illegal. Before buying, check your home country's customs regulations.

EMBASSIES AND CONSULATES

UK (Gran Canaria)	USA (Gran Canaria)	Ireland (Gran Canaria)	Australia (Madrid)	Canada (Madrid)
928 262 508	928 222 552	928 297 728	91 353 6600	91 423 3250

Useful Words and Phrases

Spanish (**español**), also known as Castilian (**castellano**) to distinguish it from other tongues spoken in Spain, is the language of the Canary Islands. The islanders' version has a sing-song quality more reminiscent of the Spanish spoken in Latin America than the mainland.

GREETINGS AND COMMON WORDS

Do you speak English? **¿Habla inglés?**
I don't understand **No entiendo**
I don't speak Spanish **No hablo español**
Yes/No **Sí/no**
OK **Vale/de acuerdo**
Please **Por favor**
Thank you (very much) **(Muchas) gracias**
You're welcome **De nada**
Hello/Goodbye **Hola/adiós**
Good morning **Buenos días**
Good afternoon/evening **Buenas tardes**
Good night **Buenas noches**
How are you? **¿Qué tal?**
Excuse me **Perdón**
How much is this? **¿Cuánto vale?**
I'd like... **Quisiera/me gustaría**

EMERGENCY!

Help! **¡Socorro!/¡Ayuda!**
Could you help me please? **¿Podría ayudarme por favor?**
Could you call a doctor please? **¿Podría llamar a un médico por favor?**

DIRECTIONS AND TRAVELLING

Aeroplane **Avión**
Airport **Aeropuerto**
Car **Coche**
Boat **Barco**
Bus **Autobús/guagua**
Bus stop **Parada de autobús**
Station **Estación**
Ticket (single/return) **Billete (de ida/de ida y vuelta)**
I'm lost **Me he perdido**
Where is...? **¿Dónde está...?**
How do I get to...? **¿Cómo llego a...?**
 the beach **la playa**
 the telephone **el teléfono**
 the toilets **los servicios**
Left/right **Izquierda/derecha**
Straight on **Todo recto**

ACCOMMODATION

Do you have a single/double room available?
 ¿Tiene una habitación individual/doble?
 with/without bath/toilet/shower
 con/sin baño/lavabo/ducha
Does that include breakfast?
 ¿Incluye el desayuno?
Could I see the room?
 ¿Puedo ver la habitación?
I'll take this room **Cojo esta habitación**
One night **Una noche**
Key/Lift **Llave/Ascensor**
Sea views **Vistas al mar**

DAYS

Today **Hoy**
Tomorrow **Mañana**
Yesterday **Ayer**
Later **Más tarde**
This week **Esta semana**
Monday **Lunes**
Tuesday **Martes**
Wednesday **Miércoles**
Thursday **Jueves**
Friday **Viernes**
Saturday **Sábado**
Sunday **Domingo**

NUMBERS

1 **uno**	11 **once**	21 **veintiuno**	200 **doscientos**
2 **dos**	12 **doce**	22 **veintidós**	300 **trescientos**
3 **tres**	13 **trece**	30 **treinta**	400 **cuatrocientos**
4 **cuatro**	14 **catorce**	40 **cuarenta**	500 **quinientos**
5 **cinco**	15 **quince**	50 **cincuenta**	600 **seiscientos**
6 **seis**	16 **dieciséis**	60 **sesenta**	700 **setecientos**
7 **siete**	17 **diecisiete**	70 **setenta**	800 **ochocientos**
8 **ocho**	18 **dieciocho**	80 **ochenta**	900 **novecientos**
9 **nueve**	19 **diecinueve**	90 **noventa**	1000 **mil**
10 **diez**	20 **veinte**	100 **cien**	

Useful Words and Phrases

RESTAURANT

I'd like to book a table
Quisiera reservar una mesa
A table for two please
Una mesa para dos, por favor
Could we see the menu, please?
¿Nos trae la carta, por favor?
What's this? **¿Qué es esto?**
A bottle/glass of... **Una botella/copa de...**

Could I have the bill please?
¿La cuenta, por favor?
Service charge included **Servicio incluido**
Waiter/waitress **Camarero/a**
Breakfast **Desayuno**
Lunch **Almuerzo**
Dinner **Cena**
Menu **La carta**

MENU READER

a la plancha grilled
aceite oil
aceituna olive
agua water
ajo garlic
almendra almond
anchoas anchovies
arroz rice
atún tuna

bacalao cod
berenjena aubergines
bistec steak
bocadillo sandwich

café coffee
calamares squid
cangrejo crab
carne meat
cebolla onion
cerdo pork
cerezas cherries
cerveza beer
champiñones mushrooms
chocolate chocolate
chorizo spicy sausage
chuleta chop
conejo rabbit
cordero lamb
crema cream
crudo raw
cubierto(s) cover (cutlery)
cuchara spoon
cuchillo knife

embutidos sausages
ensalada salad

entrante starter
espárragos asparagus

filete fillet
flan crème caramel
frambuesa raspberry
fresa strawberry
frito fried
fruta fruit

galleta biscuit
gambas prawns
gazpacho andaluz gazpacho (cold soup)
guisantes peas

habas broad beans
helado ice cream
hígado liver
huevos fritos/revueltos fried/scrambled eggs

jamón serrano ham (cured)
jamón York ham (cooked)
judías beans
judías verdes French beans
jugo fruit juice

langosta lobster
leche milk
lechuga lettuce
legumbres pulses
lengua tongue
lenguado sole
limón lemon

lomo de cerdo pork tenderloin

mantequilla butter
manzana apple
mariscos seafood
mejillones mussels
melocotón peach
melón melon
merluza hake
mero sea bass
miel honey

naranja orange

ostra oyster

pan bread
papas arrugadas Canarian-style boiled potatoes
patata potato
patatas fritas chips
pato duck
pepinillo gherkin
pepino cucumber
pera pear
perejil parsley
pescado fish
pez espada swordfish
picante hot/spicy
pimientos red/green peppers
piña pineapple
plátano banana
pollo chicken
postre dessert
primer plato first course
pulpo octopus

queso cheese

rape monkfish
relleno filled/stuffed
riñones kidneys

salchicha sausage
salchichón salami
salmón salmon
salmonete red mullet
salsa sauce
seco dry
segundo plato main course
solomillo de ternera fillet of beef
sopa soup

té tea
tenedor fork
ternera beef
tocino bacon
tortilla española Spanish omelette
tortilla francesa plain omelette
trucha trout

uva grape

verduras green vegetables
vino blanco white wine
vino rosado rosé wine
vino tinto red wine
zanahorias carrots

Road Atlas

For chapters: see inside front cover

Key to Road Atlas

FV-2	Motorway
	Dual carriage way
FV-10	Thoroughfare
	Main Road
	Secondary road
	Dirt road
	Lane
	Path
	Road under construction / development
x x x x	Road closed to vehicles
	Tunnel
	Ferry
	National park; Nature Reserve
	Restricted area
★	TOP 10
33	Don't Miss
22	At Your Leisure

✈	International airport
⚓ ⛵	Harbour; Marina
	Windsurfing; Catamaran sailing
	(Swimming) beach
	Monastery; Church, chapel
	Castle, Fortress; Ruin
	Radio or TV tower; Lighthouse
★	Point of interest; Archaeological sites
▲)(∩	Peak; Pass; Cave
	Lay-by; Petrol station
	Golf course; Windmill
	Campground; Lookout point; Oasis
i ✚	Information; Hospital
M	Museum; Theatre; Monument
✡ ✉	Police station; Post office
	Bus station; Bus stop
P P	(Multi-storey) Car park; Parking spaces

1 : 175 000

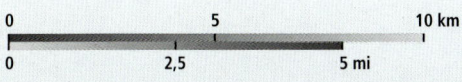

0 — 5 — 10 km
0 — 2,5 — 5 mi

Map Grid

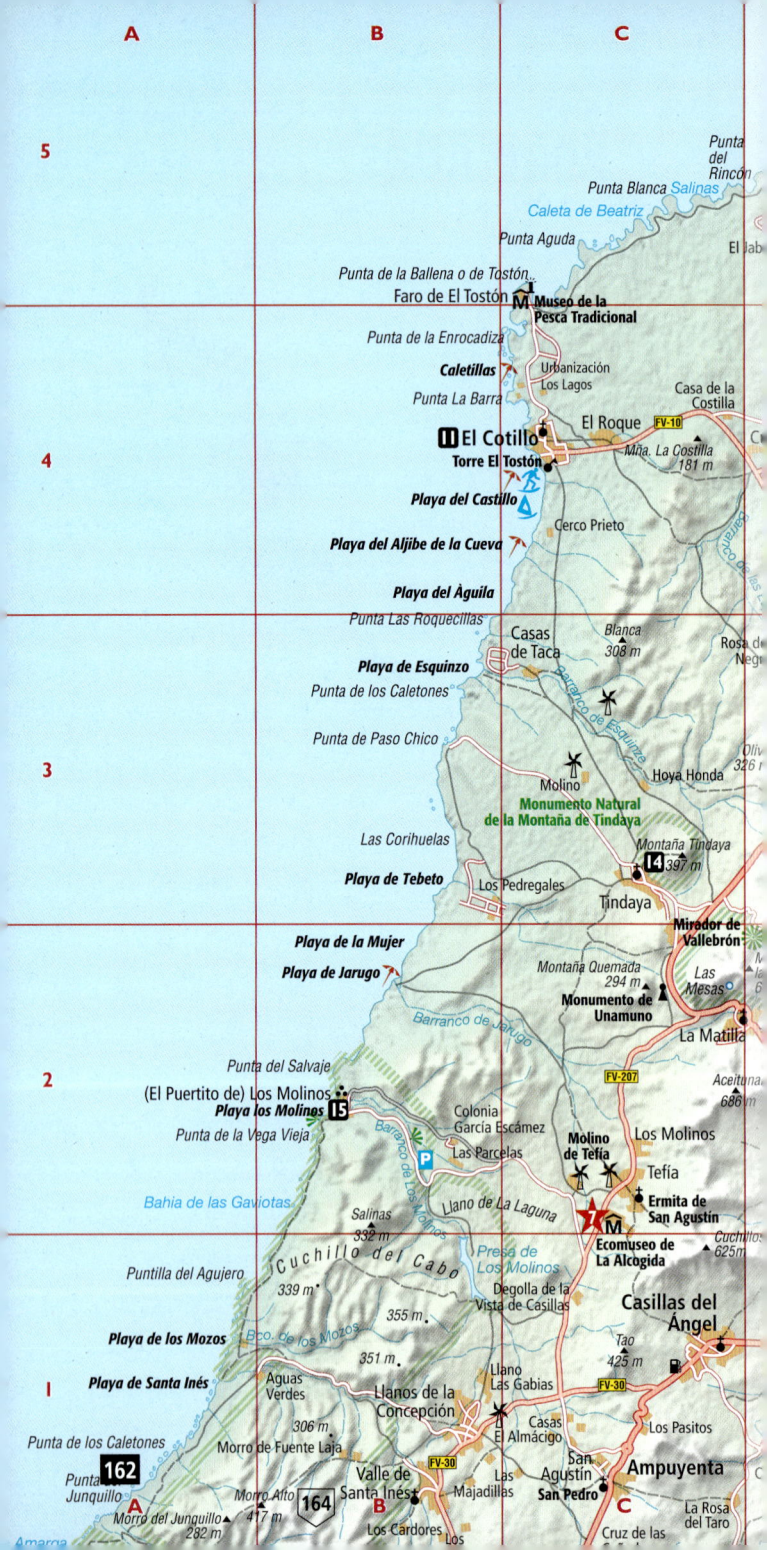

	A	B	C
5			Punta del Rincón · Punta Blanca · Salinas · Caleta de Beatriz · Punta Aguda · El Jab...
4		Punta de la Ballena o de Tostón · Faro de El Tostón · Punta de la Enrocadiza · Caletillas · Punta La Barra · El Cotillo · Torre El Tostón · Playa del Castillo · Playa del Aljibe de la Cueva · Playa del Àguila	Museo de la Pesca Tradicional · Urbanización Los Lagos · El Roque · Casa de la Costilla · FV-10 · Mña. La Costilla 181 m · Cerco Prieto
3		Punta Las Roquecillas · Playa de Esquinzo · Punta de los Caletones · Punta de Paso Chico · Las Corihuelas · Playa de Tebeto	Casas de Taca · Blanca 308 m · Rosa de Neg... · Molino · Hoya Honda · Monumento Natural de la Montaña de Tindaya · Montaña Tindaya 397 m · Los Pedregales · Tindaya · Oliv... 326 m
2		Playa de la Mujer · Playa de Jarugo · Punta del Salvaje · (El Puertito de) Los Molinos · Playa los Molinos · 15 · Punta de la Vega Vieja · Bahía de las Gaviotas · Barranco de Jarugo	Montaña Quemada 294 m · Monumento de Unamuno · Las Mesas · La Matilla · FV-207 · Aceitun... 686 m · Colonia García Escámez · Las Parcelas · Molino de Tefía · Los Molinos · Tefía · Ermita de San Agustín · Llano de La Laguna · Salinas 332 m · Presa de Los Molinos · Degolla de la Vista de Casillas · Ecomuseo de La Alcogida · Casillas del Ángel · Cuchillo... 625 m
1	Playa de los Mozos · Playa de Santa Inés · Punta de los Caletones · Punta Junquillo · 162 · A · Morro del Junquillo 282 m	Puntilla del Agujero · Cuchillo del Cabo · 339 m · 355 m · 351 m · Aguas Verdes · 306 m · Morro de Fuente Laja · Morro Alto 417 m · 164 · Valle de Santa Inés · Los Cárdores · B	Bco. de los Mozos · Llanos de la Concepción · Las Majadillas · Casas El Almácigo · FV-30 · San Agustín · San Pedro · Tao 425 m · Llano Las Gabias · FV-30 · Los Pasitos · Ampuyenta · La Rosa del Taro · Cruz de las... · C

D
E
F
Punta Martiño
Faro Martiño
Playa del Sobrado
Isla de Lobos
127 m
Playa La Arena
Parque Natural
Centro de Interpretación
El Puertito
Punta de la Vera
Playa del Bajo de la Burra
Playa de Majanicho
Punta de la Tiñosa
El Río
Punta de Corralejo
Corralejo
Majanicho
Montaña la Mancha 151 m
Punta Priela
Playa de La Concha
Flag Beach
El Jablito
Baku Water Park
Solyplayas
Playa de El Burro
Malpaís de Bayuyo
Bayuyo 269 m
Grandes Playas
Calderón Hondo 278 m
103 m
Playa Bajo Negro
Montaña Colorada 244 m
FV-101
Roya del Cura
El Jable
Playa del Moro
Culata de Roque
12
Lajares
FV-109
Parque Natural de Corralejo
Casas de Arriba
Peña Azul
Playa del Porís
Ermita de San António de Padua
Coto de los Apartaderos
Barca Quebrada
Barranco de las Lajas
Los Risquetes
Casilla de Costa
Monumento Natural del Malpaís de La Arena
Rosa de los Negrines
Arena 420 m
Cueva del Llano
La Rosita
328 m
Caletón de las Palomas
Roja 312 m
Villaverde
13
Rosa Erguida
Playa La Cazuela
FV-10
FV-1
La Oliva
6
Aljibe
El Sobaco
Oliva 326 m
Montaña de Escanfraga 531 m
Casa Mané
Las Portadas
Parque Holandés
El Jablito
Museo del Grano La Cilla
Casa de los Coroneles
Bco. del Cabadero
Horno de Cal
Playa del Chinchorro
FV-102
Morro de los Rincones 510 m
Rosa del Podenco
Aljibe
Punta del Tarajalito
Caldereta
Casas El Jablito
FV-102
Playa del Perchel
Vallebrón
Bco. de Tinojay
Majada del Caballo
Las Llanadas
Montaña de la Muda 689 m
553 m
Paisaje Protegido de Vallebrón
Punta del Bajo de Tío Viña
Guisguey
Vega Nueva
Casa de la Tia Cristina
El Time
Punta la Tiñosa
FV-214
FV-10
Temejereque 511 m
Ermita de las Mercedes
Punta de la Pared
Casas de Felipito
Puerto Lajas
Playa de Lajas
Tamariche
Las Majadas
La Herradura
Bco. de la Monja
Punta del Roque
Tetir
La Asomada
Aeropuerto Abandonado
La Caldereta 395 m
Los Estancos
Rosa de la Monja
Cortijo de la Sargenta
Rosa de las Arenas
La Rosa de la Villa
Punta de las Arenas
Montaña de Tesjuates 443 m
16
Puerto del Rosario
342 m
FV-20
FV-3
Casa Museo Unamuno
Tesjuates
Zurita 275 m
El Espino Gordo
Bco. de Río Cabras
Playa Blanca
FV-225
Presa de Rio Cabras
Antiguo Parador Nacional
259 m
Punta de Piedra Cal
Playa Blanca
Cercado Viejo
165
Punta del Viento
Rosa del Taro
Aeropuerto
5
4
3
2
1

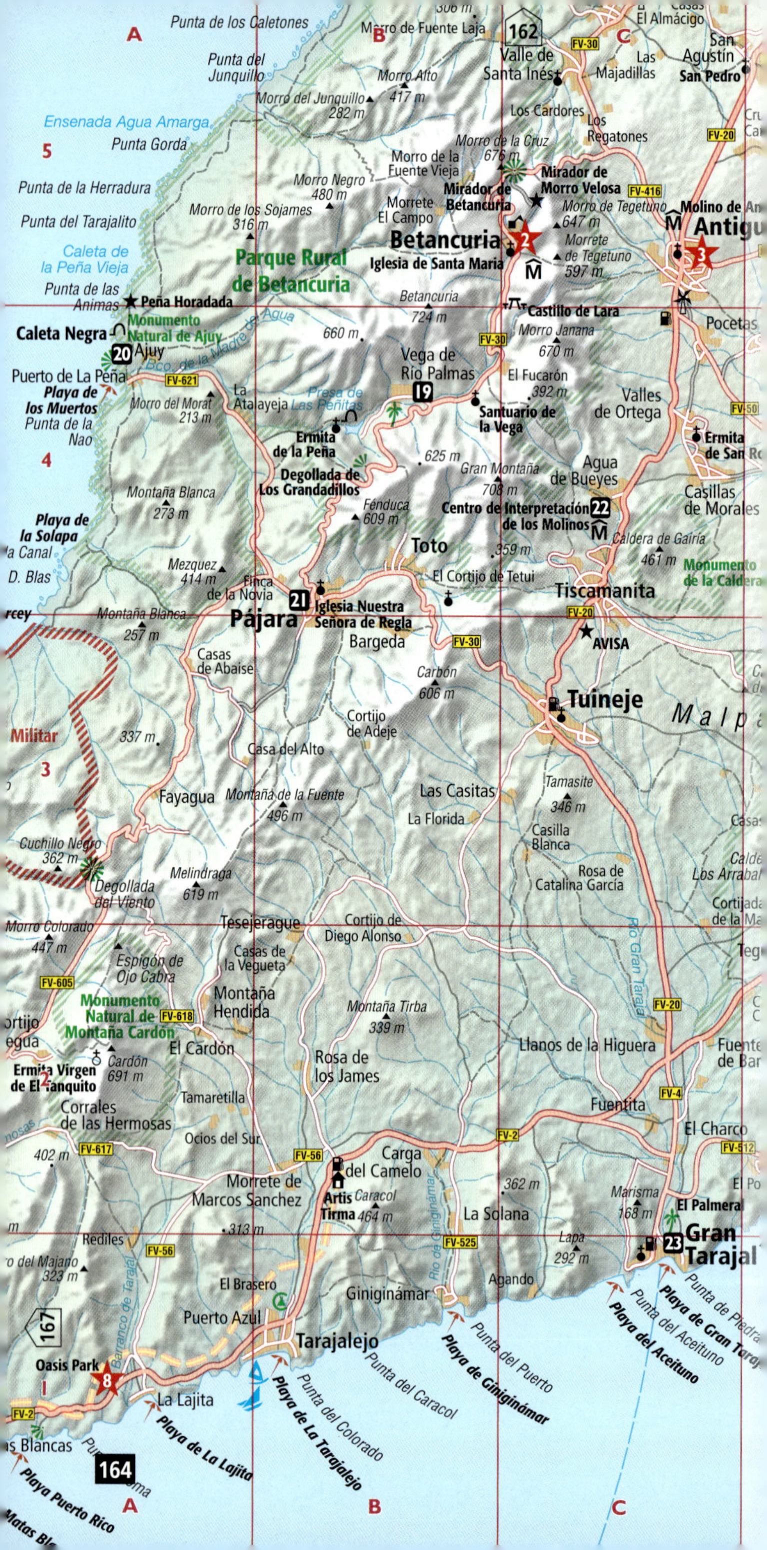

Los Pasitos
FV-225
Presa de Rio Cabras
163
259 m
Antiguo Parador Nacional
Punta de Piedra Cal
Ampuyenta
Cercado Viejo
Playa Blanca
La Rosa del Taro
Punta del Viento
Aeropuerto de Fuerteventura
Cruz de las Cañadas
Rosa del Taro 593 m
Cuchillo de Palomares
Punta Gonzalo
FV-2
Playa del Matorral
Triquivijate
El Matorral
de Antigua
Montaña del Negrito 282 m
Playa de las Caletitas
FV-413
Finca del Saladar
Barranco de la Muley
Casa de Pancho Sarabia
Nuevo Horizonte
Cuchillete de Buenavista
Caleta de la Camella
Ermita de San Francisco
Morro de la Degollada del Fronton 416 m
232 m
Montaña Blanca de Abajo 192 m
17 Caleta de Fuste
Castillo San Buenaventura
Puerto del Castillo
Playa del Castillo
FV-50
Corrales de Miraflor
Playa de La Guirra
Majada Blanca
San Roque
Caleta de La Guirra
Finca del Vicario
Bco. de la Torre
Museo de la Sal
124 m
Salinas del Carmen 18
Playa de Las Salinas
Agudo 494 m
Playa del Muellito
Puerto de la Torre
263 m
Caleta de la Ballena
Morro Halcones 428 m
Granja Experimental
Caldera de la Laguna
FV-420
Punta del Viento
Pozo Negro
Playa Pozo Negro
Punta Medina
La Atalayita
436 m
Paisaje Protegido del Malpaís Grande
Playa de los Vallichuelos
Casas de Ezquén 201 m
Tecinosquey
Bco. Valle de la Cueva
Playa de la Cueva
Los Toneles
Ensenada de Toneles
Caldera Arrabales
FV-2
Caldera de Jacomar 436 m
Casas de Jacomar
Teguital
Morro del Peñon 398 m
Ensenada de Puerto Rico
Punta Las Borriquillas
Monumento Natural de los Cuchillos de Vigán
Ensenada de Valle Corto
Casas de la Cañada de Teguital
Bco. de Gran Valle
Fuente de Bartolo
Vigán 468 m
Punta del Jurado
La Entallada
Playa de los James
340 m
FV-512
Las Playitas
185 m
Peñon del Roque
23
El Poris
Punta de la Entallada
Costa de la Entallada
Playa de Las Playitas
Playa de los Pobres
Piedras Caidas o Morro de Cran Tarajal
D
E
F
5
4
3
2
1

A B C

5

4

3

2

Playa de Barloven

Casa Agua Melianes
El Islote

Morro del Joar
621 m

Punta de
El Pesebre
Caleta de
la Madera
Punta
de Barlovento
Roque del Moro
Playa de
Cofete
Villa Winter
Pico de la Manta
643 m

Punta Cotillo
o de Cachorros
Las Talabijas
189 m
Casas y Manantial
del Mosquito
El Golfo
28 Cofete
Pico de la Zarza
807 m

Playa
de Ojos
**Mirador de
Barlovento**
Fraile
683 m
**Degollada
de Cofete**
485 m

Las Pilas
Cuchillo del Palo
441 m
424 m
Casas de Gran Valle

Las Salinas
Morro Mungla
390 m
Corral Bermejo
335 m

Puerto
de la Cruz
La Rajila
Casas de Jorós
(z. Zt. gesch

1
Faro de Jandía
Playa de los Pilas
Baja Gómez
Casa de
la Señora
Cantil

Punta de Jandía
Punta del Viento
Morro
Jable
27

166
Playa
Motor

A B C

D
E
F
Playa de Garcey
Montaña E
257 m
La Matanza
Las Salinas
Zona Militar
337 m
5
Vigocho
382 m
Las Salinas
Cuchillo Negro
362 m
Bco. Amanay
Punta Amanay
Degollada del Viento
306 m
Morro Colorado
447 m
Espig Ojo Ca
FV-605
Punta de las Goteras
Monument Natural de Montaña Car
Playa de Terife
Cortijo de Chilegua
Playa Negras
Ermita Virgen de El Tanquito
4
Cardón
691 m
Playa de Ugán
Corrales de las Hermos
Bco. de las Hermosas
Puerto Nuevo
402 m
FV-617
164
Punta de Guadalupe
La Pared
24
Playas de La Pared
Playa del Viejo Rey
195 m
Rediles
Morro del Majano
323 m
Agua Liques
Barranco de Tarajal
Granillo
123 m
Oasis Park
3
8
Agua Tres Piedras
Istmo de La Pared
FV-2
Matas Blancas
Punta Paloma
Parque
Playa Puerto Rico
Playa de Matas Blancas
25
Costa Calma
Punta de los Molinillos
Punta Paloma
Punta de Playa Larga
Playa Larga
158 m
1
Playas de Jandía
Natural
Loma Negra
335 m
FV-2
Los Gorriones
Casas de Pecenescal
Playa Barca
Morro de la Burra
515 m
Barranco del Valluelo
El Paso
253 m
Playas de Sotavento
2
621 m
Montaña Blanca
394 m
Bco. del Salmo
Casas Risco del Paso
de Jandía
Bco. los Canarios
Risco del Paso
Casas de Mal Nombre
Jandía
Casas de Esquinzo
Boca de Mal Nombre
Monte del Mar
Playa de Esquinzo
Aguda
255 m
FV-602
Esquinzo
Butihondo
Playa de Butihondo
I
26
Jandía
Humedal Saladar de Jandía
Punta del Matorral o del Morro Jable
Playa del Matorral
D
E
F

Lanzarote

Atlantic Ocean

La Isleta
La Santa
El Cuch
Playa Teneza
Playa de la Madera
Los Islotes
Tajaste
Tinajo
Guiguan
Baja de la Piedra Dorada
Mancha Blanca
La Vegue
El Volcán
Tinguatón
Parque Nacional de Timanfaya
Caldera Colorada 465 m
Montañas del Fuego
San Ba
Masdache
El Golfo
Islote de la Vega
Vegas de Tegoyo
El Golfo
La Geria
Playa de Montaña Bermeja
Yaiza
El Tablero
La Asomada
Conil
Salinas de Janubio
Las Hoyas
Uga
El Mesón
Mácher
Atalaya de Femés 608 m
Las Casitas de Femés
Las Breñas
Puerto del Car
Atlante del Sol
Femés
Playa Quemada
El Rubicón
Bahía de Ávila
El Veril Atravesado
Los Ajaches
Playa Blanca

168

Playas del Papagayo
Playa de Puerto Muelas

D
E
F
Isla de Montaña Clara
Caletón Oscuro
5
Pedro Barba
Isla Graciosa
El Río
Caleta del Sebo
Mirador del Río
34
Órzola
Malpaís de la Corona
Yé
Las Rositas
Los Molinos
4
Cueva de los Verdes
35
Casas Las Escamas
Jameos del Agua
10
Máguez
Risco de Famara
Los Picachos
33
Haría
Playa de Famara
Bajamer
Santa Sport
Arrieta
La Caleta
Peñas del Chache
671 m
Casa del Molino
El Cangrejo
Sóo
Risco de las Nieves
Los Valles
Mala
Cuchillo
Las Laderas
36
Jardín de Cactus
Muñique
Guatiza
3
El Mojón
Teguise
Tiagua
29
Teseguite
Playa de Tic Joaquín
Nazaret
Tao
El Jable
Urbanización Las Cabreras
Mozaga
Tahíche
San Bartolomé
Fundación César Manrique
32
El Charco
Montaña Blanca
Urbanización Costa Teguise
Argana Alta
Arrecife
2
37
Tías
Playa Honda
Castillo de San Gabriel
Arrecife (ACE)
Playa de Guasimeta
Urbanización Los Pocillos
Carmen
Atlantic Ocean
1
D
E
F

170

Las Palmas

0 — 300 m
0 — 300 yd

LUGO

José Ramírez Bethencourt
Luis Doreste Silva
15 Quince de Noviembre
León y Castillo
Galo Ponte
Plaza de la Feria
Plaza Fuente Luminosa
Monumento P. Galdós
Comandancia de Marina
Gobierno Civil
Dr. Waksman
Emilio Arrieta
Avenida Marítima
GC-1

SAN ROQUE

Obispo Rabadán
Tomás de Iriarte
Canalejas
Núñez Bosque
Murga
Plaza Padre Hilario
Venegas
León y Castillo
Cebrián
Alfonso Alvarado
Emilio Arrieta
Centro Insular Deportes
Cámara de Comercio

ARENALES

Eusebio Navarro
Clínica Balmes Cajal
Jaime Cajal
Pedro de Vera
Cebrián
Canalejas
Perojo
Colmenares
Venegas
Muelle de Las Palmas
Parque San Telmo
Ermita de San Telmo
Avenida Rafael Cabrera
Estación de Guaguas
Paseo de San Telmo

TRIANA

Bravo Murillo
Plaza del Pino
Cabildo Insular
Buenos Aires
Viera y Clavijo
Triana
Paseo Seco
Avenida Primero de Mayo
Domingo J. Navarro
Dr. Juan Padilla
San Bernardo
Pedromo
Villavicencio
Constantino
Travieso
Arena
Matula
Casas Metián & Negrín
Francisco Gourie
Munguia
Avenida Rafael Cabrera

Galería de Arte
Casa-Museo Benito Pérez Galdós

General Bravo
Torres Clavel
Cano
Losero
Plaza Stagno
F. Jareño
Teatro Pérez Galdós

San Francisco
Malteses
Gabinete Literario
Plaza Cairasco
Lentini
Plaza Mercado
Mercado de Vegueta **41**

Remedios
M. H. de Mendoza (Plaza Hurtado)
Pelota
Botas
Calvo Sotelo
Obispo Matarero
Ermita de San Antonio Abad
Audiencia

Teatro Guiniguada
Casa de Colón
Palacio Episcopal
Casa Regental
Catedral Santa Ana
39
42 MCAAM
Museo Diocesano
J. León y Joven
Espíritu Santo
Palacio de Justicia

Casa Consistorial
Plaza Espíritu Santo
Casa Viera y Clavijo
Museo Canario **40**
García Tello
Luis Millares
Reloj
Doctor Chil
Agustín Millares
Juan E. Doreste
Avenida Marítima
GC-1

LA VEGUETA **171**

Islas Canarias

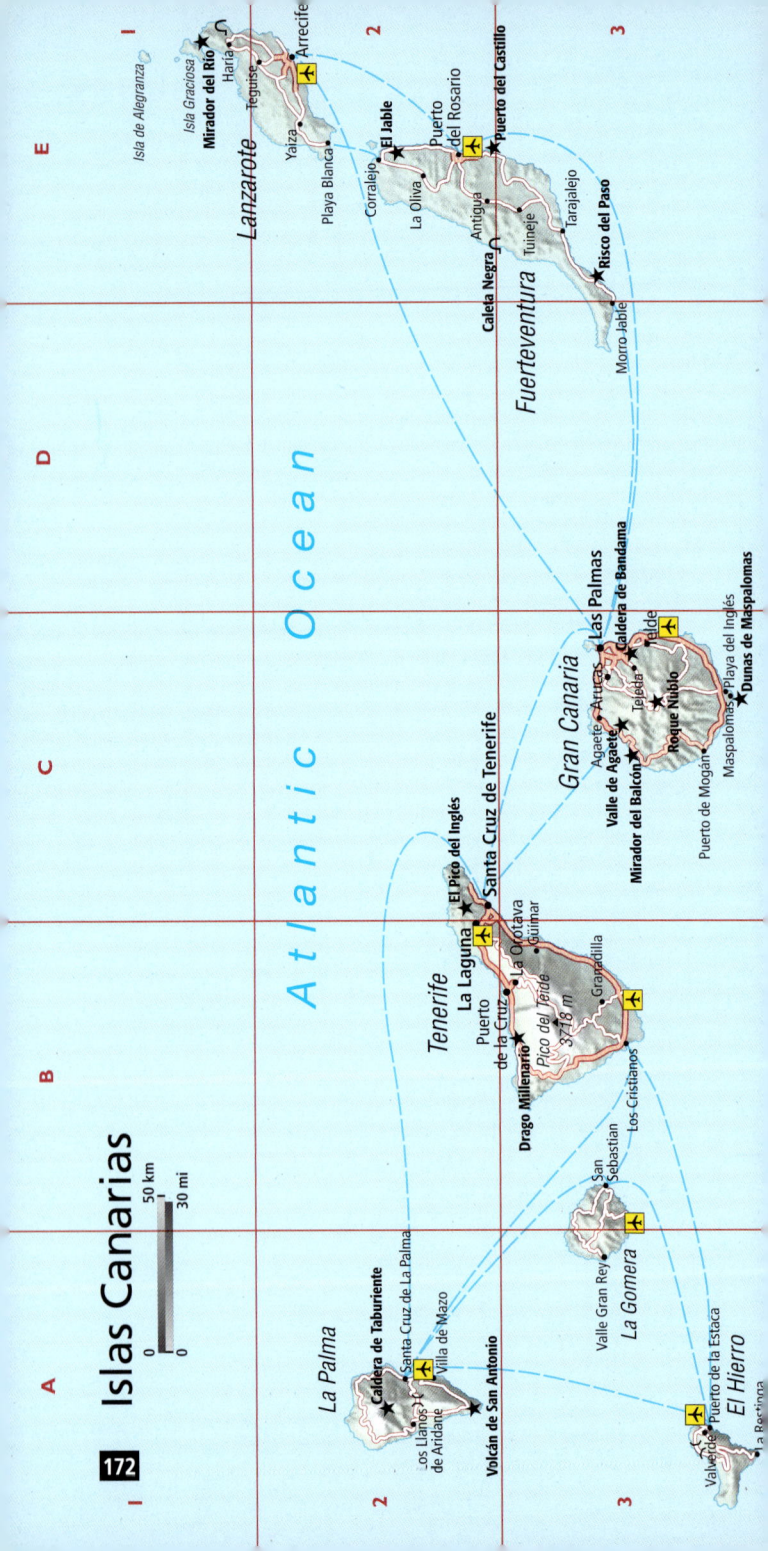

Index

A
accommodation 38, 61–62, 82, 103–104
Agua Tres Piedras 152
airports and air services
  Fuerteventura 36, 155
  Gran Canaria 128
air travel 36, 128, 155
Ajuy 77
  Caleta Negra 77
  eating out 81
aloe vera 11, 41
Antigua 37, 73
  accommodation 82
  eating out 79
  Molino de Antigua 73, 148
  Nuestra Señora de Antigua 73
aquarium 76, 84
architecture 51, 56, 96, 132, 136
Arrecife
  Castillo de San Gabriel 123
  Castillo de San José 123
  Iglesia de San Ginés 123
Arrecife, Lanzarote 123
arrival 36, 155
ATM (cashpoint) machines 155
Ayoze, King 14

B
Baku 27, 50
Baku Water Park 50
banks 155
Barlovento 91
barrancos (ravines) 10
bars 42
beaches 51
  Caleta de Fuste 76
  Cofete 99
  Corralejo 51
  Costa Calma 90
  El Cotillo 55
  Flag Beach, Corralejo 52
  Glass Beach, Corralejo 52
  Jandía Playa 91, 96
  Morro Jable 97
  Playa de Cebada 97
  Playa de Famara 119
  Playa del Castillo 55
  Playa de los Lagos 56
  Playa de Sotavento 91, 96
  Playa Galera 51
  Playa la Concha 49
  Playa Matorral 96
  Playas de Jandía 90
Betancuria 15, 21, 28, 37, 70–72, 147
  Casa Santa María 71, 83
  Convento de San Buenaventura 72
  eating out 79
  Iglesia de Santa María 71
  Museo Arqueológico 72
  Museo Artesanía 71, 79
  Museo de Arte Sacro 71
Béthencourt, Jean de 13–15, 70
bike hire 64
birdlife 141
boat trips *see* sea travel
bodyboarding 26, 64
Botanic Garden, La Lajita 95
bowling 27, 51
The Burial of the Sardine 20
buses
  Fuerteventura 37, 108, 114
  Gran Canaria 128–129

C
cactus gardens
  Betancuria 79
  Lanzarote 122
  La Oliva 53
  Villa Verde 56
Café El Naufragio 33
Café El Naufragio, Puerto del Rosario 33
Caleta de Fuste 26, 27, 30, 37, 75
  accommodation 82
  eating out 80
Caleta Negra, Ajuy 77
camels, camel rides 28–29, 94, 95, 114
car hire
  Fuerteventura 36, 37
  Gran Canaria 108
Carnaval 19–21, 129
Casa Cuartel, Teguise 118
Casa de Colón, Las Palmas de Gran Canaria 132
Casa del Capellán, La Oliva 54
Casa de los Coroneles, La Oliva 53
Casa Mané, La Oliva 54
Casa-Museo Dr Mena, La Ampuyenta 148
Casa Museo Unamumo, Puerto del Rosario 75
Casa Santa María, Betancuria 71, 83
Casas de los Volcanes, Lanzarote 117
casas rurales 39
Casillas del Angel 148
Castillo de San Gabriel, Arrecife 123
Castillo de San José, Arrecife 123
Castillo de Santa Barbara, Lanzarote 119
catamaran trips 48, 64, 106, 108
Catedral de Santa Ana, Las Palmas de Gran Canaria 134
caves
  Caleta Negra 77
  Cueva del Llanos 56
  Cueva de los Verdes 117, 122
  Cueva Pintada 133
  Cueva Villaverde 56
  Jameos del Agua 116
  Los Hervideros 120
Centro Atlántico de Arte Moderno (CAAM), Las Palmas de Gran Canaria 132
Centro de Arte Canario (CAC), La Oliva 53, 145
Centro de Interpretación de los Molinos 78, 148
Charco de los Clicos 120
children's activities 26–27, 158
  Baku Water Park 50
  beach at Caleta de Fuste 76
  beaches 27
  Caleta Negra, Ajuy 77
  camel rides 114
  Cueva del Llanos 56
  Cueva de los Verdes 122
  Ecomuseo de La Alcogida 74
  kite flying 27
  La Lajita Oasis Park 93
  Molino de Antigua 73
  Oceanarium Explorer 84
  Playa de los Lagos 56
  Playa la Concha 49
  scuba-diving 27
  Subcat (submarine trip) 106
  surfing 26
  Taberna Fogalera 59
  windsurfing 26
climate & season 39, 108, 129, 154
cochineal 122
Cofete 98–99
Coffee 40
Columbus, Christopher 132
concessions 158
consulates and embassies 158
Convento de San Buenaventura, Betancuria 72
Convento de San Francisco, Teguise 119
Convento de Santo Domingo, Teguise 119
Corralejo 11, 12, 16, 17, 18, 19, 21, 26, 27, 30, 34, 36, 50–52, 142, 145
  accommodation 61
  Baku 27
  Baku Water Park 50
  eating out 58
  El Hotel del Terror 51
  Flag Beach 52

173

Index

Glass Beach 52
International Kite Festival 27
Parque Natural de las Dunas de Corralejo 52
Playa Galera 51
Villa Tabaiba Galeria de Arte 51
Costa Calma 27, 90, 96, 150
 accommodation 103
 eating out 100
credit cards 155
crime 157
Cueva del Llanos, Villaverde 56
Cueva de los Verdes, Lanzarote 117, 122
Cueva Villaverde 56
currency 155
customs regulations 41, 158

D

Degollada de los Granadillos 148
dental services 158
disability, travelling with a 158
dolphin watching 30
drinking water 40, 158
driving 37
drugs and medicines 158

E

eating out 40, 58–60, 78, 79–81, 98, 100–102, 124–125, 135
Echadero de los Camellos, Lanzarote 114
Ecomuseo de La Alcogida 12, 74, 146
El Cotillo 12, 15, 21, 26, 27, 32, 55
 accommodation 62
 eating out 59
electricity 156
El Golfo, Lanzarote 120
El Hotel del Terror, Corralejo 51
El Muelle, Isla de Lobos 138
El Puertito, Isla de Lobos 48, 49, 138
El Río 121
Embalse de la Peñitas 77
embassies & consulates 158
embroidery 42, 56, 63
emergencie telephone numbers 157
entertainment 42, 64, 84
Ermita de La Virgen de la Peña 77
Ermita de San Pedro de Alcántara 148
Esquinzo 96
 accommodation 104
 eating out 101

F

farming 11
Faro de Entallada 78
Faro de Lobos 140
Faro de Morro Jable 97
ferries 36, 108, 155
festivals & events 19–21, 42, 129
 The Burial of the Sardine 20
 Fiesta de Nuestra Señora de la Candelaria 54
 Kite Festival 27, 51
fishing 11, 30, 32, 106
Flag Beach, Corralejo 18, 52
food and drink 22–25, 39–41
 see also eating out
 coffee 40
 drinking water 40, 158
 goat's cheese 23, 25, 83
 specialities 23, 25, 83
 tapas 23, 40
foreign exchange 155
Fortaleza/Torre del Tostón, El Cotillo 55
fuel 38
Fundación César Manrique, Lanzarote 120
FV Massira 32

G

gifts & souvenirs 41–42
Glass Beach, Corralejo 52
goats 28–29
goat's cheese 25, 83
gofio 24, 28
go-karting 84
golf 42, 84
Gran Canaria *see* Las Palmas de Gran Canaria
Gran Tarajal 37
Guanches 13–15, 28, 53, 56
Guize, King 14, 53

H

Hammer, Jo 55
Haría
 Museo de Arte Sacro 121
Haría, Lanzarote 121
health 158
history 13–15, 21
los hornitos 48, 140
horseriding 84
hoteles rurales 39
hotels 39 *see also* accommodation

I

The Idol of Tara 15
Iglesia de Nuestra Señora de Guadalupe, Teguise 118
Iglesia de Nuestra Señora de la Candelaria, La Oliva 54
Iglesia de San Ginés, Arrecife 123
Iglesia de Santa María, Betancuria 71
Iglesia Nuestra Señora del Rosario 75
insurance 38, 154
Inter-island travel 155 *see also* ferries, sea travel
International Kite Festival, Corralejo 27
Isla de Lobos 27, 31, 48–49, 138–141
 El Muelle 138
 El Puertito 49, 138
 Faro de Lobos 49, 140
 Las Lagunitas 48, 139
 Montaña de la Caldera 141
Isla la Graciosa 121

J

Jameos del Agua, Lanzarote 116–117
Jandía Playa 11, 14, 16, 31, 32, 37, 90–92, 91, 96
 accommodation 103
 eating out 101
 Faro de Morro Jable 97
 Villa Winter 99
Jardín de Cactus, Lanzarote 122
jetfoil service 98

K

kiteboarding 16–18, 42, 64
kite flying 27

L

La Ampuyenta
 Casa-Museo Dr Mena 148
 Ermita de San Pedro de Alcántara 148
La Geria, Lanzarote 120
Lajares 56, 142
 accommodation 62
 eating out 60
 School of Embroidery 56
La Lajita 93–95
 Botanic Garden 95
 eating out 100
La Lajita Oasis Park 93–95
Lanzarote 107–126
 Arrecife 123
 Casas de los Volcanes 117
 Castillo de Santa Barbara, Teguise 119
 Convento de San Francisco, Teguise 119
 Convento de Santo Domingo, Teguise 119
 Cueva de los Verdes 117, 122
 eating out 124–125

174

Index

Echadero de los Camellos 114
El Golfo 120
Fundación César Manrique 120
Haría 121
Iglesia de Nuestra Señora de Guadalupe, Teguise 118
Jameos del Agua 116
Jardín de Cactus 122
La Geria 120
Mirador del Río 121
Museo Internacional de Arte Contemporáneo 123
Palacio del Marqués 119
Palacio Spínola, Teguise 118
Parque Nacional de Timanfaya 114–115
Playa de Famara 119
Puerto del Carmen 123
Ruta de los Volcanes 115
shopping 126
Teguise 118–119
Timple Museum, Teguise 118
La Oliva 53–54, 145
 cactus garden 53
 Casa de los Coroneles 53
 Casa Mané 54
 Centro de Arte Canario (CAC) 53
 eating out 60
 Museo del Grano La Cilla 54
La Pared 14, 26, 96
 eating out 100
La Rosita 56–57
Las Lagunitas, Isla de Lobos 139
Las Palmas de Gran Canaria 127–178
 Casa de Colón 132
 Catedral de Santa Ana 134
 Centro Atlántico de Arte Moderno (CAAM) 132
 eating out 135
 Mercado de Vegueta 134
 Museo Canario 133
 Museo Pueblo Canario 134
 Parque de San Telmo 134
 shopping 136
Las Playitas
 eating out 81
locusts 12
Los Boquetes 152
Los Hervideros 120
Los Molinos 75
 eating out 80

M
majoreros 6, 10, 13
malpaís 143
Manrique, César 54, 108, 114, 116, 121

markets 42, 63, 83, 105, 118, 123, 126
Martínez, Tinín 34
Maxorata, King 14
menu reader 160
Mercado de Vegueta, Las Palmas de Gran Canaria 134
Mirador del Río, Lanzarote 121
Mirador de Morro Veloso 147
mojo 22
Molino de Antigua 73, 148
Montaña Colorada 142, 144
Montaña de la Caldera, Isla de Lobos 141
Montaña Tindaya 15, 57, 145
Morro Jable 21, 27, 29, 30, 31, 37, 91, 97
 accommodation 104
 eating out 102
Museo Arqueológico, Betancuria 15, 70, 72
Museo Artesanía, Betancuria 71, 79
Museo Canario, Las Palmas de Gran Canaria 133
Museo de Arte Sacro, Betancuria 71
Museo de la Sal 76
Museo del Grano La Cilla, La Oliva 54
Museo Internacional de Arte Contemporáneo, Arrecife 123
Museo Pueblo Canario, Las Palmas de Gran Canaria 134

N
national holidays 156
nightlife 42, 64, 84, 106
Nuestra Señora de Antigua 73
Nuestra Señora de la Regla, Pájara 77

O
off-road driving 38, 91, 92, 97, 99
opening hours 41, 156

P
Pájara 77, 148
 accommodation 82
 eating out 81
Palacio del Marqués, Lanzarote 119
Palacio Spínola, Lanzarote 118
papas arrugadas 22
paragliding 16
Parque de San Telmo, Las Palmas de Gran Canaria 134
Parque Eólico Cañada de la Barca 11
Parque Nacional de Timanfaya, Lanzarote 114–115

Parque Natural de las Dunas de Corralejo 52
passports and visas 154
personal safety 157
Pico de la Zarza 98
Playa Barca
 accommodation 104
Playa de Cebada 97
Playa de Famara, Lanzarote 119
Playa de la Caleta, Isla de Lobos 49, 141
Playa de la Concha, Isla de Lobos 141
Playa de Sotavento 91
Playa la Concha 49
 Playa de la Caleta 141
 Playa la Concha 49
Playa Matorral 96
Playas de Jandía 90–92
post offices 157
Puerto del Carmen, Lanzarote 123
Puerto del Rosario 75
 Café El Naufragio 33
Puerto Del Rosario
 eating out 80

R
resorts 36
restrooms 158
Ruta de los Volcanes, Lanzarote 115

S
Salinas del Carmen 76
Salinas Del Carmen
 eating out 80
scuba-diving 27, 31, 42, 84, 106
sea travel 36, 48, 64, 84, 106, 108, 155
Sendero de Bayuyo 142–144
shipwrecks 32–33
shopping 41–42, 63, 83, 105, 109, 126, 136
snorkelling 31
squirrels 29, 152
SS American Star 33, 78
stamps 157
surfing 17, 42, 52, 64
swimming 150

T
tapas 22, 23, 40
taxis 37, 129
Teguise, Lanzarote 118–119
 Casa Cuartel 118
 Convento de San Francisco 119
 Convento de Santo Domingo 119

Index / Picture Credits

Iglesia de Nuestra Señora de Guadalupe 118
Palacio del Marqués 119
Palacio Spínola 118
Timple Museum 118
tennis 106
time differences 155, 156
Timple Museum, Teguise 118
Tindaya mountain 15, 57, 145
tipping 157
Torre del Tostón, El Cotillo 55
tourist information 36, 108, 128, 154–155
travel documents 154
trike tours 84
Tuineje 21

U
Unamuno, Miguel 76
Unamuno, Miguel de 146
useful words and phrases 159–160

V
Valle de Santa Inés 147
Vega de Río Palmas 21, 76, 77
Vega De Río Palmas
eating out 81
Villa Tabaiba Galeria de Arte 51
Villaverde 15, 56, 145
accommodation 62
cactus garden 56
eating out 60
Villa Winter, Jandía Playa 99
Volcan de Bayuyo 145

W
wakeboarding 16
walking & hiking 64, 106, 115, 138, 142–144, 150–152
whale watching 30
windmills 10, 56, 73, 78, 148
windsurfing 16, 26, 42, 52, 64, 84, 90, 106
wine 109
Winter, Gustav 99

Picture Credits

AA/Pete Bennett: 128, 129

AA/Steve Day: 17 (bottom), 18 (bottom), 68, 69, 92 (bottom), 109, 121, 122, 141, 150

AA/Clive Sawyer: 22, 24 (top), 66, 77, 110, 123, 130

AA/James A. Tims: 4, 8, 18 (top), 19 (left), 19 (centre), 19 (right), 20 (bottom), 24 (2nd from bottom), 27, 28, 29 (bottom), 31, 32, 33 (left), 33 (right), 34, 44, 46, 47, 48, 51, 52, 53, 54, 56, 57, 71, 73, 76, 86, 87, 90, 93, 94 (top and bottom), 95, 96, 97, 99, 112, 113, 140, 144

AA/Steve Watkins: 30

DuMont Bildarchiv: 15

DuMont Bildarchiv/Sabine Lubenow: 10, 12, 24 (bottom), 49, 50, 55, 72, 74, 75, 78, 88, 92, 98, 115, 119, 138, 145, 149

DuMont Bildarchiv/Olaf Lumma: 17 (top), 26, 70, 117, 118

DuMont Bildarchiv/Hans Zaglitsch: 20 (top), 21, 132

laif: 114

laif/Naftali Hilger: 116

laif/Gunnar Knechtel: 24 (2nd from top)

laif/Fluvio Zanettini: 14, 133

LOOK-foto/age fotostock: 7

LOOK-foto/Jürgen Richter: 11, 25

mauritius images/Alamy: 29 (top)

mauritius images/United artists: 152

On the cover: huber images: Reinhard Schmid (top and bottom), getty images (background)

Credits

1st Edition 2015

Worldwide Distribution: Marco Polo Travel Publishing Ltd
Pinewood, Chineham Business Park
Crockford Lane, Chineham
Basingstoke, Hampshire RG24 8AL, United Kingdom.
© MAIRDUMONT GmbH & Co. KG, Ostfildern

Authors: Paul Murphy, Rolf Goetz
Editor: Dina Stahn, Stuttgart
Revised editing and translation: Jon Andrews, jonandrews.co.uk
Program supervisor: Birgit Borowski
Chief editor: Rainer Eisenschmid

Cartography: © MAIRDUMONT GmbH & Co. KG, Ostfildern
All rights reserved. No part of this book may be reproduced, stored in a retrieval system or transmitted in any form or by any means (electronic, mechanical, photocopying, recording or otherwise) without prior written permission from the publisher.

Printed in China

Despite all of our authors' thorough research, errors can creep in. The publishers do not accept any liability for this. Whether you want to praise us, alert us to errors or give us a personal tip – please don't hesitate to email or post:

MARCO POLO Travel Publishing Ltd
Pinewood, Chineham Business Park
Crockford Lane, Chineham
Basingstoke, Hampshire RG24 8AL
United Kingdom
Email: sales@marcopolouk.com

FSC
www.fsc.org
MIX
Paper from responsible sources
FSC® C020056

10 REASONS
TO COME BACK AGAIN

1. The **best climate in the world** is worth a trip at any time of the year.

2. The **beautiful sandy beaches** offer a wealth of possible activities.

3. After doing the **surf course** for beginners, you want to put your expert skills to the test.

4. Away from the beach **new, well-marked trails** make you want to go hiking.

5. There are no doubt a lot of new **family additions to the Oasis Zoo**.

6. The traditional **fish restaurants on the waterfront** are always so inviting.

7. You won't find anywhere else where the *papas arrugadas con mojo verde* taste better.

8. The **sunset** over the Atlantic Ocean will enchant you again and again.

9. There is also a lot to explore on Fuerteventura's **neighbouring islands**.

10. The Canarian **way of life** demands to be celebrated with the locals at the village fiestas.